College Students' Perceptions of Libraries and Information Resources

A Report to the OCLC Membership

A Companion Piece to *Perceptions of Libraries and Information Resources*

College Students' Perceptions of Libraries and Information Resources

A Report to the OCLC Membership

Principal contributors

Cathy De Rosa, M.B.A., Vice President, Marketing and Library Services

Joanne Cantrell, Marketing Analyst

Janet Hawk, M.B.A., Manager, Market Research & Analysis

Alane Wilson, M.L.I.S., Senior Library Market Consultant

Graphics, layout and editing

Brad Gauder, Senior Marketing Writer

Andy Havens, Manager, Creative Services

Rick Limes, Art Director

Sam Smith, Art Director

The full report titled *Perceptions of Libraries and Information Resources* is available at:
http://www.oclc.org/reports/2005perceptions.htm

OCLC Online Computer Library Center, Inc.
Dublin, Ohio USA

Table of Contents

Introduction		**vii**
Part 1:	**Libraries and Information Sources—** **Use, Familiarity and Favorability**	**1-1**
	1.1 Library Use	1-1
	1.2 Familiarity with and Usage of Multiple Information Sources	1-4
	1.3 How Respondents Learn about New Information Resources	1-8
	1.4 Impressions of Information Sources	1-10
Part 2:	**Using the Library—In Person and Online**	**2-1**
	2.1 Activities at the Library	2-1
	2.2 Awareness of Library Electronic Resources	2-3
	2.3 Using Library Electronic Information Resources	2-5
	2.4 Seeking Assistance in Using Library Resources	2-6
	2.5 Familiarity with the Library Web Site	2-8
	2.6 The Internet Search Engine, the Library and the Librarian	2-9
	2.7 Keeping Up-to-Date with Library Resources	2-15
Part 3:	**The Library Brand**	**3-1**
	3.1 The Value of Electronic Information Resources	3-2
	3.2 Judging the Trustworthiness of Information	3-3
	3.3 Trust in Library Resources and Search Engines	3-4
	3.4 Free vs. For-Fee Information	3-6
	3.5 Validating Information	3-9
	3.6 Libraries—Positive and Negative Associations	3-12
	3.7 Lifestyle Fit	3-19
	3.8 Books—the Library Brand	3-22
	3.9 Brand Potential—Libraries, Books and Information	3-27
Part 4:	**College Students' Advice to Libraries**	**4-1**
	4.1 College Student View: The Library's Role in the Community	4-2
	4.2 Rating Library Services	4-4
	4.3 Advice to Libraries	4-5
Part 5:	**Perceptions of Potential College Students**	**5-1**
Conclusion		**6-1**
About OCLC		**7-1**

Appendix A, including the methodology and supporting tables, is available at www.oclc.org/reports/perceptionscollege.htm

Introduction

OCLC produced this report to focus on the perceptions college students have of libraries and information resources. It is a subset of the December 2005 OCLC Perceptions of Libraries and Information Resources *report.*

The 396 college students who participated in the survey range in age from 15 to 57 and are either undergraduate or graduate students. The college students were from all of the six countries included in the survey. Responses from U.S. 14- to 17-year-old participants have been included to provide contrast and comparison with the college students, as these young people are potential college attendees of the future.

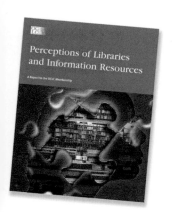

The full report, Perceptions of Libraries and Information Resources, *is available at* http://www.oclc.org/reports/2005perceptions.htm.

In 2003, OCLC published *The 2003 OCLC Environmental Scan: Pattern Recognition* as a report to the OCLC membership to identify and describe issues and trends that are impacting and will impact OCLC and, in particular, libraries. The goal of the report was first to inform OCLC's key decision makers to guide them in strategic planning and later to serve as a reference document for librarians as they work on strategic planning for their institutions and communities.

In the introduction to the *Scan* (page ix), we wrote: "It has become increasingly difficult to characterize and describe the purpose of using libraries [...] The relationships among the information professional, the user and the content have changed and continue to change." Another way of stating this is that trends indicate a dissonance between the environment and content that libraries provide and the environment and content that information consumers want and use. Three major trends were identified in the *Scan* that provide evidence of that dissonance. Self-service, satisfaction and seamlessness seem to exemplify the expectations of the information consumer in the huge "infosphere" in which libraries operate. The characteristics that support self-service, satisfaction and seamlessness, such as ease of use, convenience and availability, appeared to many information professionals, including the authors of the *Scan,* to be as important to the information consumer as information quality and trustworthiness.

The *Scan* provides references to studies, articles and reports that support the identification and analysis of these overarching trends. But, few of these resources emanated from the part of the infosphere that OCLC and libraries inhabit and there are no major recent empirical studies that look specifically and broadly at the role libraries and librarians play in the infosphere, from the point-of-view of the information consumer. How are libraries perceived by today's information consumer? Do libraries still matter? On what level? Will library use likely increase or decrease in the future?

As a consequence, early in 2005, OCLC Market Research staff, with input from many other OCLC staff and hundreds of librarians who have contributed to discussions and workshops, conceived of a project designed to better understand these trends as they relate to libraries and the information consumer. To that end, OCLC commissioned Harris Interactive Inc., a company that for 45 years has provided custom research to a broad range of clients including nonprofit organizations and governmental agencies, to administer the resulting survey on behalf of OCLC.

We were clear as to the goals of the survey. We wanted to know more about people's information-seeking behaviors, how familiar people are with the variety of e-resources libraries provide for their users and how libraries fit into the lives of the respondents. One of the most important goals of the project as a whole was to collect information that would help us build a better understanding of the "Library" brand.

The topics explored in the survey include the perceptions and preferences of information consumers; users' relationships with and use of libraries, including usage of and familiarity with electronic information resources; awareness of libraries and resources offered; the "Library" brand and its ubiquity and universality; trust of libraries and their resources; and people's perceptions of the library's purpose/mission.

We wanted to survey a broad set of information consumers. Our goal was to gather survey data across a wide range of age groups and geographic regions. We also wanted to understand more about college students as information consumers, both inside and outside the United States. Although respondents were not selected on the basis of their participation in post-secondary education, they were asked to indicate their level of educational attainment and if they were currently attending a postsecondary institution. Three hundred and ninety-six out of the total 3,348 indicated they were currently college students. This report presents the data and comments gathered from these respondents.

Given budget constraints and geographic reach goals, the survey was administered electronically and in English.

Methodology in brief

Perceptions of Libraries and Information Resources is an OCLC-commissioned blind survey of information users from Harris Interactive Inc.

- **Survey conducted**: May 20–June 2, 2005.
- **3,348 respondents** completed the survey, including 396 college students and 621 U.S. 14- to 17-year-olds.
- Survey was conducted in **English**.
- **Ages represented**: 14 to 65 and older.
- Mix of **male and female** respondents.
- **Geography**: Australia, Canada, India, Singapore, the United Kingdom (U.K.) and the United States (U.S.).
- **Survey completed online**; respondents are at least familiar with online resources and have access to the Internet.
- The collected data have an overall statistical **margin of error of +/- 1.69 percent** at the 95 percent confidence level for the online population in the countries surveyed.
- **"College students"** is used in the report to refer to postsecondary students, both graduate and undergraduate; these students reside in all geographic regions surveyed.
- Data for college students are often presented in comparison with data for the total respondents, but it is important to note that the data for students is a subset of the data for all respondents.
- Percentages in data tables may not total 100 percent due to rounding, because respondents frequently were asked to select all responses that apply or because respondents were not required to answer the question.
- Several of the following parts include samples of the verbatim comments. The comments are included as written by the survey respondents, including misspellings and grammatical errors.

A complete description of the methodology is available in the online appendix to this report at:
www.oclc.org/reports/perceptionscollege.htm

All respondents therefore use the Internet, are at least somewhat familiar with using electronic Web resources and took the survey in English. Respondents could have taken this survey in a library that provides Internet access, as some respondents indicated they access the Internet via the library.

We understand that the results, therefore, represent the online population, a subset of library users. Please read the survey results with this in mind. We did. We are also mindful that the survey respondents do represent a significant, and potentially growing, percent of library and potential library users. As outlined more fully in the Methodology section of the full report, the survey was weighted demographically and fairly represents the online population of all countries surveyed except India, due to low sample size.

Recent surveys report that over 60 percent of the populations of Australia, Canada, Singapore, United Kingdom and United States have Internet access and the growth in Internet access over the last five years is staggering. Most countries surveyed have seen an increase in Internet access of 50 to 100 percent. Information consumers are using the Internet more—both at the library and elsewhere.

As is the case with the full *Perceptions* report, the findings presented in this report do not surprise, they confirm. During the hundreds of *Scan* discussions and meetings held over the past 24 months, themes surfaced. "Users are as comfortable using Web information sources as library sources." Our study shows this perception to be true, across countries, across U.S. age groups, across library card holders and non-card holders, and across college students. "The library brand is dated." Again, our survey findings do not surprise, they confirm. One difference did surface in the data about respondents currently attending college: they are more aware of and use libraries' information resources more than other survey respondents. In addition, the more educated the respondents, the more they continue to use libraries after graduation.

Trends toward increased information self-service and seamlessness are clearly evident in the full survey results and in this subset of results. Libraries' mindshare in this new self-service e-resource environment is also clear: behind newer entrants and suffering a lack of differentiation from search engines. College students and U.S. 14- to 17-year-old respondents use libraries more than total respondents, although many of them use the library less since they began using the Internet. Both groups are more aware of libraries' electronic resources than total respondents, but awareness does not translate into high usage. Overall, respondents have positive, if outdated, views of the "Library." Younger respondents—teenagers and young adults—do not express such positive associations as frequently.

Our collective challenge is, therefore, to take this information—both the positive and the challenging—and evaluate where to invest more, invest less, invent new and invert old, communicate more and market better.

Cathy De Rosa
Vice President, Marketing & Library Services

Part 1: Libraries and Information Sources—Use, Familiarity and Favorability

96%

have visited a public library.

Survey results indicate a high level of both use of and familiarity with a wide variety of information resources. Eighty-seven percent of college students have visited a college library in person, while almost all college student respondents have visited a public library in person. Sixty-one percent of college students surveyed have used a library Web site. Ninety percent of college student respondents hold a library card.

College student respondents' familiarity with electronic information resources varies. Like the total respondents, college students are very familiar with e-mail, search engines and online news.

While most electronic resources, from e-mail to online databases to audiobooks, are used by a portion of all survey respondents, frequency of use is clearly dominated by three resources: e-mail, search engines and instant messaging. Eighty-nine percent of college students typically begin their information search using a search engine.

61%

have used a library Web site.

Favorability of information sources is similar to the data related to familiarity, with search engines again dominating as the favored choice. Seventy-two percent of college student respondents said the search engine would be their first choice the next time they need a source for information.

Half of the college student respondents anticipate their library use will remain flat in the next three to five years. Forty-four percent of college student respondents say that their library use has increased in the past three to five years, while 38 percent anticipate their use will increase in the next three to five years.

90%

hold a library card.

1.1 Library Use

Survey results generally indicate a higher level of information resource use among college students than among total respondents.

Eighty-seven percent of college students have visited a college library in person, and more than half (57 percent) have visited an online college library (Web site). Ninety-six percent of both total respondents and college student respondents have visited a public library in person. Visits to the online public library were substantially lower, at 39 percent for college students and 27 percent for total respondents.

Ninety percent of college students hold a library card, while 72 percent of total respondents hold a library card. College students use both college and public libraries frequently. Sixty-five percent of college students use their college library at least monthly, while 40 percent use a public library at least monthly.

The survey asked respondents if their usage increased or decreased in the last three to five years. Forty-four percent of college students indicate that their library usage has increased, while 25 percent of total respondents report their library usage has increased. Sixteen percent of students say their library use has decreased in the past three to five years, while 31 percent of total respondents report their library use has decreased in the same time period.

Respondents also were asked to project the level of future library usage. Half of the college students anticipate their library use will remain the same. Thirty-eight percent of college students projected increased library usage, compared to 20 percent of total respondents.

Public and College Library Usage and Percent of Library Card Holders—
by College Students and Total Respondents

	College Students	Total Respondents
Percent of library card holders	90%	72%
Visited a public library in person	96%	96%
Visited an online public library (Web site)	39%	27%
Visited a college library in person	87%	57%
Visited an online college library (Web site)	57%	22%

Source: *Perceptions of Libraries and Information Resources*, OCLC, 2005, questions 805 and 815.

Frequency of Library Use—*by College Students*

How frequently do you go to each of the following libraries?
(Only college/university library and public library included below.)

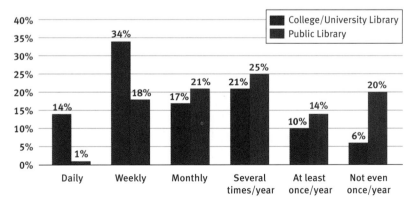

Source: *Perceptions of Libraries and Information Resources*, OCLC, 2005, question 820.

> **50%**
> *anticipate that library use will remain flat in the future.*

Frequency of Library Use—
by College Students and Total Respondents

How frequently do you go to each of the following libraries?

(Only college/university library and public library included below.)

	College/University Library		Public Library	
	College Students	Total Respondents	College Students	Total Respondents
Daily	14%	3%	1%	1%
Weekly	34%	7%	18%	13%
Monthly	17%	6%	21%	19%
Several times/year	21%	14%	25%	24%
At least once/year	10%	17%	14%	16%
Not even once/year	6%	53%	20%	27%

Source: *Perceptions of Libraries and Information Resources*, OCLC, 2005, question 820.

My schedule rarely fits their schedule.

21-year-old undergraduate from the United States

Source: *Perceptions of Libraries and Information Resources*, OCLC, 2005, question 812b, "Please list two negative associations with the library."

Past and Anticipated Library Use—
by College Students

How much has your personal library use changed over the last three to five years? How do you anticipate your personal usage of the library to change over the next three to five years?

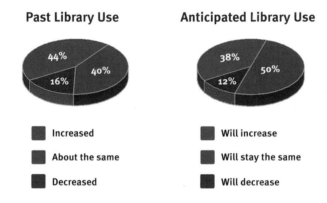

Past Library Use

- Increased
- About the same
- Decreased

Anticipated Library Use

- Will increase
- Will stay the same
- Will decrease

Source: *Perceptions of Libraries and Information Resources*, OCLC, 2005, questions 1220 and 1225.

Past Library Usage	College Students	Total Respondents	Anticipated Future Library Use	College Students	Total Respondents
Increased	44%	25%	Will increase	38%	20%
About the same	40%	44%	Will stay the same	50%	62%
Decreased	16%	31%	Will decrease	12%	18%

Source: *Perceptions of Libraries and Information Resources*, OCLC, 2005, questions 1220 and 1225.

1.2 Familiarity with and Usage of Multiple Information Sources

College students are very familiar with search engines. Fifty-eight percent are at least somewhat familiar with online libraries, significantly more than the 33 percent of total respondents.

The survey asked respondents to rate their familiarity with the following five information sources: search engines, libraries, bookstores, online libraries and online bookstores.

Seventy-two percent of college students are *extremely familiar, very familiar* or *somewhat familiar* with search engines. More than 60 percent of total respondents, regardless of geographic region, are *extremely familiar, very familiar* or *somewhat familiar* with search engines. Just 1 percent of total respondents surveyed have *never heard of* search engines, while all of the college students have heard of search engines.

In the 13 years that search engines have been in existence, they have achieved a familiarity rating that is slightly higher than that of physical libraries and considerably higher than that of online libraries.

Over a third of college students are *extremely familiar* with libraries and bookstores at 34 percent and 36 percent, respectively, compared to total respondents at 26 percent for both libraries and bookstores. College students also have a higher familiarity with online versions of libraries and bookstores than total respondents. Twenty percent of college students are *extremely familiar* with online libraries, and 25 percent of students are *extremely familiar* with online bookstores. Only 4 percent of college students *never heard of* online libraries, compared to 20 percent of total respondents.

Just remember that students are less informed about the resources of the library than ever before because they are competing heavily with the Internet.

20-year-old undergraduate from the United States

Source: *Perceptions of Libraries and Information Resources,* OCLC, 2005, question 1240, "If you could provide one piece of advice to your library, what would it be?"

45%

are extremely familiar with search engines.

34%

are extremely familiar with libraries.

Familiarity Ratings for Information Sources— *by College Students and Total Respondents*

Please rate how familiar you are with the following sources/places where you can obtain information.

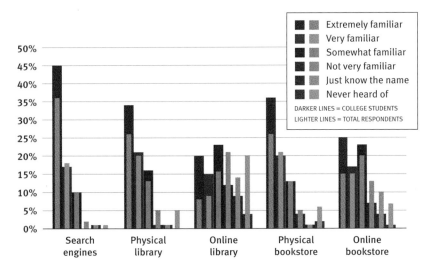

Source: *Perceptions of Libraries and Information Resources,* OCLC, 2005, question 1305.

Awareness and Usage of Electronic Resources

The majority of college student respondents have used e-mail, search engines and instant messaging.

Respondents were asked to indicate their level of awareness and usage of 16 electronic resources.

- Search engines
- Library Web sites
- Online bookstores
- Online news
- Electronic magazines/journals
- Audiobooks (downloadable/digital)
- Electronic books (digital)
- Online databases
- Topic-specific Web sites
- E-mail
- Instant messaging/online chat
- E-mail information subscriptions
- Ask an expert
- Online librarian question services
- RSS feeds
- Blogs

College student respondents show a wide familiarity with and usage of these electronic resources, including use of electronic magazines/journals, online databases and electronic books. Library Web site usage is high among college students, at 61 percent.

Total respondents also show a wide familiarity with and usage of most of these electronic resources. The use of e-mail and search engines is the highest among all resources across all segments surveyed, while all electronic resources are used by at least 5 percent of respondents.

Usage of Electronic Resources—
by College Students and Total Respondents

Please indicate if you have used the following electronic information sources, even if you have used them only once.

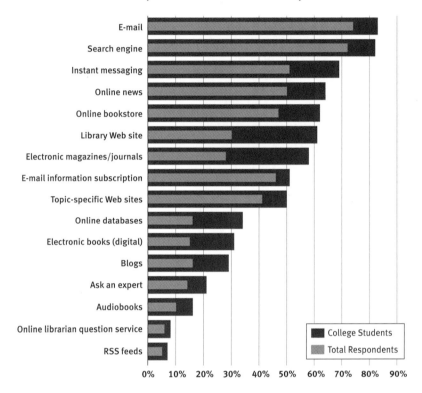

Source: *Perceptions of Libraries and Information Resources,* OCLC, 2005, question 505.

61%

have used the library Web site— two times higher than the percentage of total respondents.

Starting an Information Search

College students use search engines to begin information searches at almost the same rate as total respondents.

The survey asked respondents to indicate, from a list of the same 16 electronic resources, the electronic resource they typically use to **begin** an information search. The survey findings indicate that 89 percent of college student information searches begin with a search engine, compared to 84 percent of total respondents' searches. Library Web sites were selected by just 2 percent of students as the source used to begin an information search. Very little variability in preference exists among total respondents and college students.

Improve search engines

48-year-old undergraduate from Canada

Source: *Perceptions of Libraries and Information Resources*, OCLC, 2005, question 1240, "If you could provide one piece of advice to your library, what would it be?"

Where Electronic Information Searches Begin— *by College Students and Total Respondents*

Where do you typically begin your search for information on a particular topic?

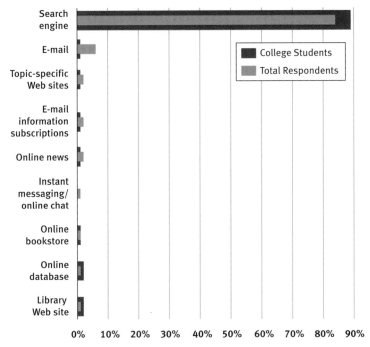

Source: *Perceptions of Libraries and Information Resources*, OCLC, 2005, question 520.
Note: Only electronic resources with usage rates of 1 percent or more are represented on this graph.

Search Engine Used Most Recently

Respondents who indicated that they use search engines were asked to identify the search engine used in their most recent search by selecting from a list of 21 brand-specific search engines. Sixty-eight percent of college students reported Google was the search engine they used most recently; Yahoo! was used by 15 percent and MSN Search was used by 5 percent. Google was used most frequently by 62 percent of total respondents. Yahoo! ranked second at 18 percent, followed by MSN Search at 7 percent and Ask.com (known as Ask Jeeves when the survey was administered) at 3 percent.

Search Engine Used Most Recently—
by College Students and Total Respondents

Earlier you stated you typically begin your search for information using search engines. Which search engine did you use for your most recent search?

Base: Respondents who begin their search using a search engine, question 520.

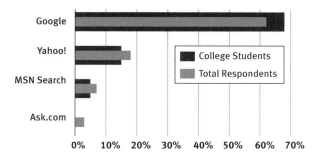

Source: *Perceptions of Libraries and Information Resources*, OCLC, 2005, question 645.

1.3 How Respondents Learn about New Information Resources

Most college students learn about new electronic information resources from friends. Thirty-three percent of college students indicate they use librarians as a resource for new electronic information—four times higher than the total respondents.

When search engines are excluded as a referral tool, most college students indicate they learn about new electronic information sources from *friends, links from electronic information sources on Web sites* or *teachers*. Sixty-seven percent of

Review the current search catalog system as it is hard to find material relevent to the topic you search for

18-year-old undergraduate from Australia

Source: *Perceptions of Libraries and Information Resources*, OCLC, 2005, question 1240, "If you could provide one piece of advice to your library, what would it be?"

college students learn about electronic information sources from *friends,* followed closely by *links from electronic information sources or Web sites,* at 61 percent. The top four mentions include:

- Friend: 67 percent
- Links from electronic information sources or Web sites: 61 percent
- Teacher: 50 percent
- News media: 44 percent

At 33 percent, college students' usage of the *librarian* as a source of information about electronic resources was the highest among all segments surveyed. Total respondents ranked the librarian as the least used source to learn about electronic information, at 8 percent.

36%
learn about new e-resources from a library Web site— more than twice the percentage of total respondents.

Learning about Electronic Information Sources— *by College Students and Total Respondents*

Other than search engines, how do you learn about electronic information sources? (Select all that apply.)

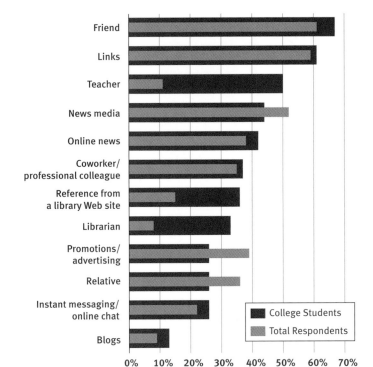

Source: *Perceptions of Libraries and Information Resources,* OCLC, 2005, question 605.

1.4 Impressions of Information Sources

The majority of college students view search engines very favorably as a source for information. Libraries and bookstores are also viewed favorably.

Search engines have the highest favorability ratings of the five information sources evaluated. The search engine is viewed as *very favorable* or *favorable* by 92 percent of college students and 88 percent of total respondents. The library is viewed as *very favorable* or *favorable* by 85 percent of college students and 79 percent of total respondents.

College students have a more favorable view of the online library than total respondents. Sixty-six percent of the college students stated that they have at least a somewhat favorable view of the online library, compared to 46 percent of total respondents.

Favorable Ratings for Information Sources— *by College Students and Total Respondents*

Based on your overall impressions, please indicate how you would rate each source/place with respect to the information available. Even if you haven't used one or more of the sources/places, rate each one based on what you have seen, read or heard about it.

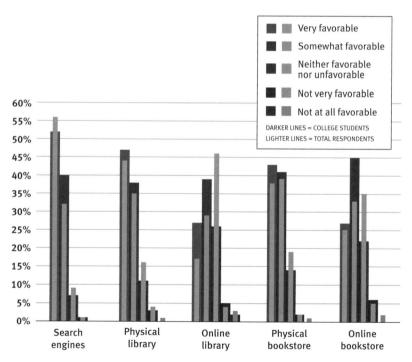

Legend:
- Very favorable
- Somewhat favorable
- Neither favorable nor unfavorable
- Not very favorable
- Not at all favorable

DARKER LINES = COLLEGE STUDENTS
LIGHTER LINES = TOTAL RESPONDENTS

Source: *Perceptions of Libraries and Information Resources*, OCLC, 2005, question 1315.

Being at University allows you membership of a large and well respected library on campus. There are librarians and other staff who can help you if you need advice, whereas searching online you cant ask anyone for help.

18-year-old undergraduate from Australia

Source: *Perceptions of Libraries and Information Resources*, OCLC, 2005, question 812a, "Please list two positive associations with the library."

Information Sources Considered

Search engines are considered most often as an information source among college students. They are also the information source most likely to be used the next time these respondents need information.

Survey respondents were asked what information sources they will consider the next time they need information. Ninety percent of college students selected search engines as an information source they would consider, while 66 percent selected the bricks-and-mortar library and 50 percent selected the online library. Ninety-one percent of total respondents selected search engines as an information source they would consider, while 55 percent selected the bricks-and-mortar library and 42 percent selected the online library.

Search engines are ranked as the "first choice" for information by 72 percent of college students, compared to 80 percent of total respondents. College students rank the library a distant second with 14 percent and the online library third at 10 percent.

First Choice for Information Source— *by College Students*

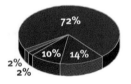

72%

10% 14%

2%
2%

- ▮ Search engines
- ▮ Library (physical)
- ▮ Online library
- ▮ Bookstore (physical)
- ▮ Online bookstore

Source: *Perceptions of Libraries and Information Resources*, OCLC, 2005, question 1335.

Information Sources Considered and First Choice— *by College Students and Total Respondents*

Next time you need a source/place for information, which source or sources would you consider? Select all that apply. And, which source/place would be your first choice?

Sources Considered	College Students	Total Respondents	First Choice	College Students	Total Respondents
Search engines	90%	91%	Search engines	72%	80%
Library (physical)	66%	55%	Library (physical)	14%	11%
Online library	50%	42%	Online library	10%	6%
Bookstore (physical)	38%	37%	Bookstore (physical)	2%	2%
Online bookstore	34%	30%	Online bookstore	2%	2%

Source: *Perceptions of Libraries and Information Resources*, OCLC, 2005, questions 1325 and 1335.

Finding Worthwhile Information

Respondents were asked to rate the information from the following brands:

- About.com
- AllTheWeb.com
- AltaVista.com
- AOL Search
- Ask an expert (e.g., Homework Helper)
- Ask.com
- Clusty.com
- Dogpile.com
- Excite.com
- Gigablast.com
- Google.com
- HotBot.com
- iWon.com
- Library Web sites
- LookSmart.com
- Lycos.com
- MSN Search
- Netscape Search
- Online librarian question services (Ask a librarian)
- Teoma.com
- Yahoo.com

Respondents who indicated any usage of the 21 brands were asked to rate the degree to which they agree or disagree that each brand they have used provides worthwhile information. College students who have used Google rate it the highest among the brands listed above; 61 percent *completely agree* Google provides worthwhile information. College students also gave the library Web site high ratings with respect to providing worthwhile information, with 45 percent who *completely agree*.

Total respondents who have used Google also rate it highest, with 55 percent indicating that they *completely agree* that Google provides worthwhile information. Yahoo! and the library Web site are closely rated by the total respondents who use those brands, at 34 percent and 33 percent respectively. MSN Search and Ask.com round out the top five brands total respondents report to provide worthwhile information.

96%

at least agree Google provides worthwhile information.

84%

at least agree library Web sites provide worthwhile information.

84%

at least agree Yahoo! provides worthwhile information.

Five Highest-Rated Information Brands with Worthwhile Information—*by College Students and Total Respondents*

Please rate the degree to which you agree or disagree that each electronic information source provides worthwhile information.

Base: Respondents who indicated usage of any of the list of 21 information brands.

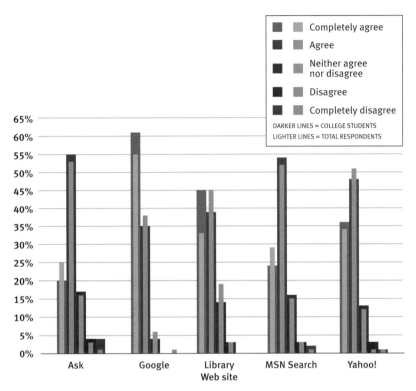

Source: *Perceptions of Libraries and Information Resources,* OCLC, 2005, question 670.

Library Electronic Resources

College student respondents who use the library agree that the library's electronic information resources are worthwhile.

Respondents who use the library's electronic information sources are in general consensus that the library sources provide worthwhile information. College students rate electronic magazines/journals, the online library catalog and reference materials highly as resources providing worthwhile information.

College students rated electronic magazines/journals highest with respect to providing worthwhile information; 85 percent *completely agree* or *agree.* The online library catalog follows closely, with 83 percent. Eighty-one percent of college students *completely agree* or *agree* that online reference materials provide worthwhile information, followed closely by the library Web site, with 79 percent who *completely agree* or *agree.*

Although usage of many of the library electronic resources is relatively low, respondents indicated that the information provided is worthwhile. While only 8 percent of college student respondents have used an online librarian question service, 64 percent of the college students who used this service *completely agree* or *agree* this service provides worthwhile information.

Part 2: Using the Library—In Person and Online

Studying

is the top library activity for college students.

In Part 1, we reviewed survey findings related to college students' frequency of use, familiarity with and favorability toward a wide range of information sources, including the physical and online library.

In Part 2, we review responses to questions that probe further for respondents' use habits regarding activities pursued at the library and through the online library. Respondents were asked about their levels of familiarity and satisfaction with library-provided electronic information resources and where they seek help when they need assistance using library information resources, as well as questions related to the evaluation of search engines and libraries against a set of performance attributes.

2.1 Activities at the Library

Monthly activity levels among college students are higher than total respondents in all but one category.

College students are more

aware

of the library's e-resources.

We asked respondents to indicate how frequently they use 20 different library resources, and we focused this section on the top eight activities. Monthly activity levels among college students are higher than total respondents in all but one category (read/borrow best-seller).

Forty-eight percent of college students report using a library to *do homework/study* at least monthly compared to 12 percent of total respondents; 45 percent report *using the computer/Internet* at least monthly compared to 13 percent of total respondents; 44 percent report *using online databases* at least monthly compared to 15 percent of total respondents; 42 percent report *researching specific reference books* at least monthly compared to 15 percent of total respondents; 39 percent report *borrowing print books* at least monthly compared to 26 percent of total respondents; 32 percent *get copies of articles/journals* at least monthly compared to 9 percent of total respondents; and 33 percent report *getting assistance with research* at least monthly compared to 11 percent of total respondents. Only 12 percent of college students report using a library to *read/borrow best-sellers* at least monthly, compared to 16 percent of total respondents.

Activities at the Library: Monthly Usage—
by College Students and Total Respondents

How frequently do you use your library for the following reasons?

Note: At least monthly is a rollup of daily, weekly and monthly.

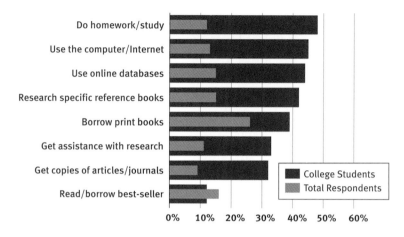

Source: *Perceptions of Libraries and Information Resources,* OCLC, 2005, question 840.

Comparing Libraries and Bookstores

College students favor libraries over bookstores for free Internet access,
free materials and special programs. They favor bookstores
for coffee shops, current materials and meeting their friends.

Respondents were asked to compare a library to a bookstore against a list of
11 activities and attributes. The data show that college students consider libraries
more suitable than local bookstores on eight of 11 activities/attributes. The highest
ratings for favoring the library for particular activities over bookstores among college
students are: free access to the Internet (94 percent), free materials (93 percent)
and access to free entertainment (85 percent). Students feel that the local bookstore
is a more suitable source than their libraries as a place for a coffee/snack shop, for
more current materials and as a place where their friends are.

Of the 11 activities listed, total respondents also feel the library is more suitable than
local bookstores in the same eight of 11 activities. Total respondents feel their library
is more suitable for providing free access to the Internet (95 percent), free materials
(95 percent) and providing special programs (89 percent).

Suitability of the Library and the Bookstore for Specific Activities—*by College Students*

Comparing the library to your local bookstore, which do you feel provides a more suitable environment for activities/materials in regard to the following?

Libraries are more suitable than bookstores for...	Bookstores are more suitable than libraries for...
Free access to the Internet: 94%	Coffee/snack shop: 86%
Free materials: 93%	More current materials: 66%
Access to free entertainment: 85%	It's where my friends are: 55%
Special programs: 78%	
Comfortable seating/meeting area: 65%	
Friendly environment: 62%	
Book club/story hour: 58%	
Access to music: 56%	

Source: *Perceptions of Libraries and Information Resources*, OCLC, 2005, question 1230.

They give people access to books that they could not afford to go to the store and buy. They allow people who can not afford a computer to use the one at the library.

22-year-old undergraduate from the United States

Source: *Perceptions of Libraries and Information Resources*, OCLC, 2005, question 812a, "Please list two positive associations with the library."

2.2 Awareness of Library Electronic Resources

Most college students are aware of library electronic resources. Awareness among total respondents is low.

Respondents were asked to indicate if their library provides various types of electronic resources. College students surveyed show high levels of awareness of library electronic resources across all eight categories. Nearly three quarters or more are aware their library has a library Web site (87 percent), an online library catalog (86 percent) and online reference materials (71 percent). Nearly half or more of college students are aware their library has electronic books (47 percent), an online librarian question service (45 percent), electronic magazines/journals (62 percent) and online databases (62 percent). The awareness of whether their library has audiobooks (downloadable/digital) is mixed, with 43 percent who are aware the library has this resource and 44 percent who are *not sure* if their library has audiobooks.

Results indicate that awareness among total respondents is low for most of the library's electronic resources. For example, 58 percent of all respondents are *not sure* if their library offers access to online databases. Of the eight library electronic resources evaluated, total respondents show the highest level of awareness for the library Web site and online library catalog, with at least 60 percent who are aware the library has these resources.

Awareness of Library Resources—
by College Students and Total Respondents

Please indicate which electronic information sources
your primary library has.

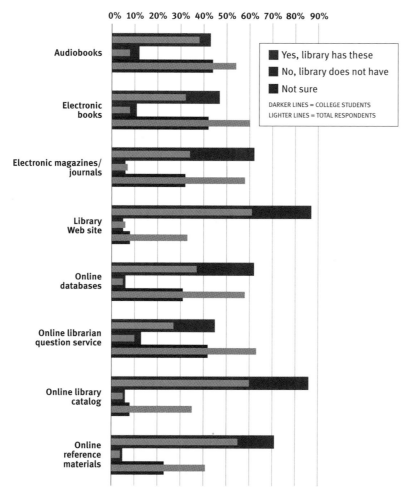

Source: *Perceptions of Libraries and Information Resources,* OCLC, 2005, question 850.

advertise to students
when they first arrive

22-year-old graduate student from the United Kingdom

Source: *Perceptions of Libraries and Information Resources,* OCLC, 2005,
question 1240, "If you could provide one piece of advice to your library,
what would it be?"

2.3 Using Library Electronic Information Resources

College students' use of library electronic resources is higher than that of overall respondents.

Use of library electronic resources among college students at least monthly is higher in all of the eight categories than that of respondents overall. Fifty-six percent of college students report using the library Web site at least monthly and 47 percent of them report using the online catalog at least monthly.

College students report low monthly use of online librarian question services and audiobooks, at 17 percent and 16 percent respectively.

Total respondents' monthly use of online databases, electronic magazines/journals, online reference materials, electronic books, online librarian question services and audiobooks is less than 20 percent in each category.

42%

use online databases at least monthly.

15%

never have used online databases.

Usage of Library Resources— by College Students and Total Respondents

Which of the following library electronic information sources have you ever used from your primary library and how often do you use them?

Base: Respondents who indicated their primary library has the following electronic information resources.

Note: At least monthly is a rollup of daily, weekly and monthly.

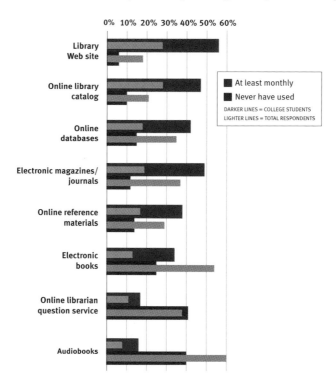

Source: *Perceptions of Libraries and Information Resources*, OCLC, 2005, question 855.

2.4 Seeking Assistance in Using Library Resources

Most respondents do not seek assistance when using library electronic resources.

Fifty-four percent of college students do not seek assistance when using library electronic resources, while 64 percent of total respondents report they have not sought help when using the library's electronic resources.

Assistance in Using the Library—
by College Students and Total Respondents

Did you ever seek help when using your library's electronic resources or when searching for information at your library?

Base: Respondents who have used the library, either walk-in or online.

	College Students	Total Respondents
Yes, have sought help when using library's electronic resources	46%	36%
No	54%	64%

Source: *Perceptions of Libraries and Information Resources,* OCLC, 2005, question 1035.

Need more staff to help people get used to the new technologies of the library

22-year-old undergraduate from the United States

Source: *Perceptions of Libraries and Information Resources,* OCLC, 2005, question 1240, "If you could provide one piece of advice to your library, what would it be?"

Sources of Help at the Library

When college students seek help at the library, librarians are the clear choice.

Of the 46 percent of college students who have sought help using the library's electronic resources, 76 percent of them indicated a *librarian* was their first choice as a source for help. Responses for sources of help were very similar among college students and total respondents.

First Source of Help at the Library—
by College Students and Total Respondents

What is the first source you typically go to for help with your problem?

Base: Respondents who sought help at the library.

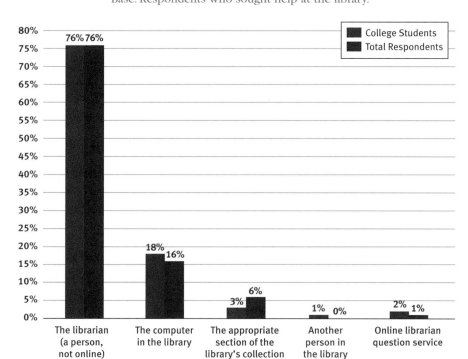

Source: *Perceptions of Libraries and Information Resources,* OCLC, 2005, question 1040.

more staff would be helpful

57-year-old graduate student from Canada

Source: *Perceptions of Libraries and Information Resources,* OCLC, 2005, question 1240, "If you could provide one piece of advice to your library, what would it be?"

2.5 Familiarity with the Library Web Site

Most college students have used a library Web site.

Respondents were asked about their familiarity with library Web sites, the main point of access to libraries' catalogs and resources. College student respondents are more familiar with library Web sites than the total respondents.

Most college students know the library Web site exists, and 35 percent are either *extremely familiar* or *very familiar* with the library Web site. Among college students who have never used an online library Web site, the main reason is that *other Web sites have better information* (44 percent). Nineteen percent of college students say they *did not know it existed or it does not exist* and 15 percent reported they *could not find the library Web site*.

For the total respondents who reported they have never visited an online library Web site, *I did not know the Web site existed/does not exist* is the primary reason cited for lack of use. Fifty-five percent of total respondents report they *did not know the library Web site exists* or say *it does not exist*.

Reasons for Never Using the Online Library Web Site—
by College Students and Total Respondents

Why haven't you ever used the online library Web site?

Base: Respondents who indicated they do not visit the library online, question 815.

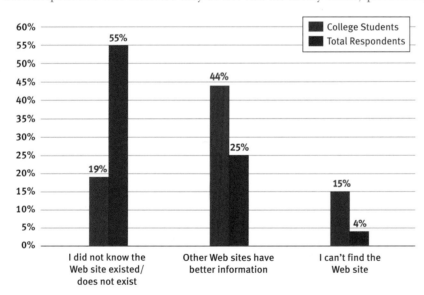

Source: *Perceptions of Libraries and Information Resources*, OCLC, 2005, question 1090.

Accessing the Library from the Web—
by College Students

Have you ever started your search for information using a search engine and ended up at a library Web site?

YES: 48% NO: 52%

If yes... did you use the library Web site?

YES: 41%

NO: 7%

If yes, did the library Web site fulfill your information needs?

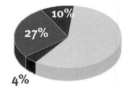

10%

27%

4%

27%: YES
but I also had to use other resources

10%: YES
the only resource I needed to use

4%: NO
not enough information available

Source: *Perceptions of Libraries and Information Resources*, OCLC, 2005, questions 1005, 1010, 1015.

2.6 The Internet Search Engine, the Library and the Librarian

Libraries are seen as more trustworthy/credible and as providing more accurate information than search engines. Search engines are seen as more reliable, cost-effective, easy to use, convenient and fast.

Earlier in this report, we reviewed data that show search engines are the preferred starting place for survey respondents when searching for information. Respondents were asked to compare search engines and libraries against a set of seven performance attributes.

Total respondents and college students rate libraries higher than search engines along two of the seven performance attributes: *trustworthy/credible sources of information* and *accurate.* Seventy-seven percent of college students and 60 percent of total respondents indicate libraries are best described using the attribute *trustworthy/credible,* while 76 percent of college students and 56 percent of total respondents indicate that libraries are best described using the attribute *accurate (quality information).*

Search engines are rated higher than libraries by total respondents and college students in five of the seven performance attributes: reliability, cost-effectiveness, ease of use, convenience and speed.

Have to actually go into the library

Takes alot of time to search

through all the books

18-year-old undergraduate from the United Kingdom

Source: *Perceptions of Libraries and Information Resources,* OCLC, 2005, question 812b, "Please list two negative associations with the library."

Attributes of the Library and Search Engine—
by College Students

Comparing an online or physical library to a search engine, please indicate which source is best described by the following:

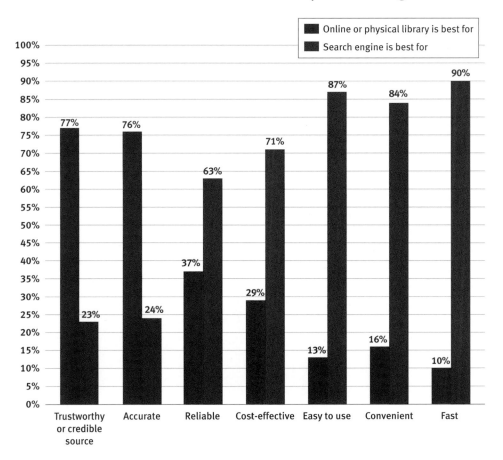

Source: *Perceptions of Libraries and Information Resources,* OCLC, 2005, question 1355.

Librarians and the Search Process

Respondents who have used a librarian for assistance agree that librarians add value to the search process.

We reviewed data reporting the percent of college student respondents who have sought help from a librarian when looking for information or using electronic information resources. Those survey respondents who have used the assistance of a librarian were also asked to rate the degree to which they agree or disagree that the librarian adds value to the search process. The data from both college students and total respondents were similar. Seventy-five percent of college students *completely agree* or *agree* that the librarian adds value to the search process, while 77 percent of total respondents *completely agree* or *agree* that the librarian adds value to the search process.

Librarian Adds Value to the Search Process—
by College Students

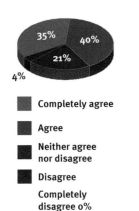

- ■ Completely agree
- ■ Agree
- ■ Neither agree nor disagree
- ■ Disagree
- Completely disagree 0%

Librarian Adds Value to the Search Process—
by College Students and Total Respondents

Please rate the degree to which you agree or disagree that the librarian adds value to the information search process.

Base: Respondents who have used a librarian for assistance.

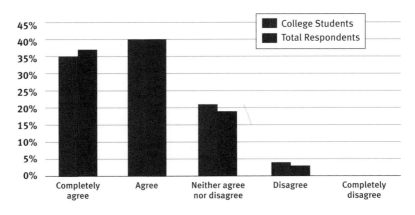

Source: *Perceptions of Libraries and Information Resources*, OCLC, 2005, question 1070.

Comparing Assistance—Search Engines and Librarians

Respondents who indicated they have used a search engine to assist in searching for information and who also indicated they have sought assistance from a librarian in the process of using library electronic resources or in searching for information were then asked to compare that assistance. Fifty-two percent of college students responded that the assistance they received from the librarian was the same as the search engine, compared to 43 percent of total respondents.

Assistance from Search Engines and Librarians—
by College Students and Total Respondents

Please compare the assistance you received from a librarian to that of the assistance from a search engine on a 5-point scale.

Base: Respondents who have used a librarian and a search engine for assistance.

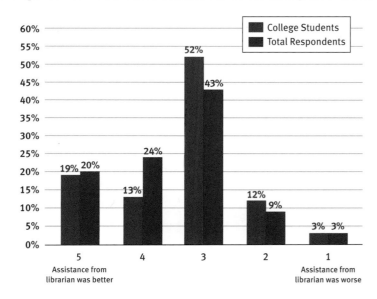

Source: *Perceptions of Libraries and Information Resources,* OCLC, 2005, question 1065.

Hire more staff to assist not just put away books.

21-year-old undergraduate from the United States

Source: *Perceptions of Libraries and Information Resources,* OCLC, 2005, question 1240, "If you could provide one piece of advice to your library, what would it be?"

Satisfaction with Search Engines and Librarians

College students are satisfied with both librarians and search engines.

Respondents who indicated they have used the assistance of a librarian and a search engine were asked to indicate their levels of satisfaction with the information provided, the quantity of information received, the speed with which the search was conducted and their overall search experience from the two sources.

Satisfaction with the Librarian and Search Engine—
by College Students

Based on the most recent search you conducted through (librarian/search engine), how satisfied were you in each of the following areas?

Base: Respondents who have used a search engine or a librarian.

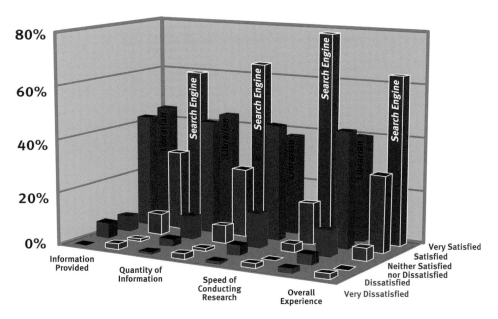

Source: *Perceptions of Libraries and Information Resources*, OCLC, 2005, questions 665 and 1050.

Satisfaction with the Information Provided

Levels of satisfaction for both the librarian and the search engine with respect to the information provided were high among college students. Eighty-eight percent of college students were *very satisfied* or *satisfied* with the information provided from their most recent search conducted with the assistance of a librarian, while 90 percent were *very satisfied* or *satisfied* with the information provided using a search engine.

The results of total respondents were similar. Eighty-eight percent of total respondents indicated they were *very satisfied* or *satisfied* with the information provided from their most recent search conducted with the assistance of a librarian. Eighty-nine percent indicated they were *very satisfied* or *satisfied* with the information provided from their most recent search using a search engine.

Satisfaction with the Quantity of Information Provided

Eighty-seven percent of college students were *very satisfied* or *satisfied* with the quantity of information provided from their most recent search using the assistance of a librarian, and 91 percent were *very satisfied* or *satisfied* with the amount of information provided in their most recent search using a search engine.

The results of total respondents again were similar. Eighty-four percent of total respondents were *very satisfied* or *satisfied* with the quantity of information provided from their most recent search using the assistance of a librarian. Eighty-nine percent of respondents indicated they were *very satisfied* or *satisfied* with the amount of information provided in their most recent search using a search engine.

Satisfaction with the Speed of Conducting the Search

Satisfaction with the speed of conducting the search is the attribute for which there is the largest difference between a search engine and a librarian. More college students are *very satisfied* with the speed of conducting the search using a search engine compared to using a librarian, 78 percent and 38 percent, respectively. When *very satisfied* and *satisfied* are combined, ratings are more similar to the speed of conducting the search using a librarian and using a search engine, 82 percent and 94 percent, respectively.

Total respondents again had similar responses. Seventy-two percent of total respondents were *very satisfied* with the speed of conducting research using a search engine, and 41 percent of total respondents were *very satisfied* with the speed of conducting research with a librarian. When *very satisfied* and *satisfied* ratings are combined, the difference is less drastic: 81 percent for a librarian vs. 92 percent for a search engine.

Satisfaction with the Overall Experience of the Search by the Librarian and Search Engine

Ninety-three percent of college students were *very satisfied* or *satisfied* with the overall experience of using a search engine, while 84 percent were *very satisfied* or *satisfied* with the overall experience of using a librarian.

Total survey respondents again responded similarly. Ninety percent of total respondents were *very satisfied* or *satisfied* with the overall experience of using a search engine. Eighty-four percent of total respondents were satisfied with the overall experience of using a librarian.

Can be hard to find good information. Slower than the internet.

20-year-old undergraduate from Canada

Source: *Perceptions of Libraries and Information Resources*, OCLC, 2005, question 812b, "Please list two negative associations with the library."

2.7 Keeping Up-to-Date with Library Resources

Nearly half of all college student respondents use the library Web site to stay current with library resources. Over a quarter do not keep up with library resources at all.

more signs

18-year-old undergraduate from the United States

Source: *Perceptions of Libraries and Information Resources*, OCLC, 2005, question 1240, "If you could provide one piece of advice to your library, what would it be?"

College students are likely to use the *library Web site*, in addition to *calling or walking in the library*, to keep up-to-date with library resources. Almost twice as many college students use the *library Web site* to keep up with resources available at the library as do all respondents, at 49 percent and 25 percent respectively.

Twenty-six percent of college students indicate they *do not keep up with resources available*. Of total respondents, 33 percent indicate they *do not keep up with resources available* at the library.

Keeping Up-to-Date on Library Resources—
by College Students and Total Respondents

How do you typically keep abreast of the resources available to you at your library? (Select all that apply.)

	College Students	Total Respondents
Library Web site	49%	25%
Call or walk in the library	48%	48%
I don't keep up with resources available	26%	33%
Point of use materials (signs/fliers/posters at the library)	25%	22%
School bulletin boards	21%	6%
E-mail lists	19%	10%
Friends/neighbors/relatives	18%	18%
Community/local paper	9%	20%

Source: *Perceptions of Libraries and Information Resources*, OCLC, 2005, question 1215.

Part 3: The Library Brand

"Books" is the library brand.

In Parts 1 and 2, we reviewed data related to college student respondents' use of libraries and their familiarity with and favorability toward a variety of information sources, including libraries and their resources. We reviewed the frequency of use of library services, how these respondents keep up-to-date with library services and their satisfaction levels with those services.

In this section, we move from reviewing usage and familiarity of information sources to reporting responses related to perceptions and trust. Ubiquitous access to content is in its infancy and there is much to learn about how people make choices and form preferences about electronic resources and services. How do college students assess and value electronic information? What, and who, do they trust? What mindshare does the "Library" hold compared to other information resources and services available to those with access to the Internet? The survey data provide some insight.

College students are looking for "worthwhile" information.

College students were asked to rate the specific criteria they used to evaluate and verify electronic resources. The top three evaluation criteria used by college students are that the source *provides worthwhile information, provides free information* and *provides credible/trustworthy information*.

All respondents, including college students, rely on themselves to judge if an electronic source is trustworthy. *Common sense/personal knowledge* is the top verification criterion among total respondents and college students. Both groups—total respondents and college students—also verify information trustworthiness based on *reputation of the company* and by *finding the information on multiple sites/cross-referencing*. Respondents believe free information is trustworthy and overwhelmingly do not trust information more if they have to pay for it. Few have paid for information.

College students trust information from both libraries and search engines.

We explored the question of product "fit" by asking respondents to tell us how well they felt different information sources fit with their lifestyle. Ease of product use and consumption or "fit" is often a key driver of both current and future use. Respondents feel search engines are a perfect fit with their lifestyle. Libraries fit but are not a perfect fit. This is true overall and for the college student subset.

We examined respondents' perceptions of the library and library information resources by asking an open-ended question about top-of-mind associations with libraries and positive and negative associations. Across all regions surveyed, respondents associate libraries first and foremost with "books." There is no runner-up. Total respondents provided thousands of positive and negative associations about libraries. Overall, respondents provided more positive than negative associations. Top positive associations are related to library products—books, materials, computers, etc. Many of the negative associations were also related to products and offerings, followed by customer/user service and facilities.

Respondents were asked what they felt was the "main purpose of the library." While about a third of total respondents and college students indicated they felt the main purpose of the library is "books," 49 percent of college students and 53 percent of all respondents feel that the library's main purpose is "information."

3.1 The Value of Electronic Information Resources

"Provides worthwhile information" is the top criterion students use when selecting electronic information. "Free" is also an important factor.

College students use multiple criteria to determine the value of electronic information sources. Contrary to what is often attributed as the primary benefit of digital information access, speed of information delivery is not the most critical factor respondents use to evaluate electronic information resources. For college students, four criteria were selected more frequently than speed. Eighty-two percent of college students typically select an information source based on whether the source *provides worthwhile information*. College students also base their decision on if the source *provides free information* (73 percent), if the source *provides credible/trustworthy information* (73 percent) and *ease of use* (64 percent).

Recommendations are used by just 36 percent of college students as a criterion for selecting an electronic information source.

To provide access to print media and electronic media.

20-year-old undergraduate from the United States

Source: *Perceptions of Libraries and Information Resources*, OCLC, 2005, question 810, "What do you feel is the main purpose of a library?"

Evaluating Information Sources—
by College Students and Total Respondents

How do you decide which electronic information source to use?
(Select all that apply.)

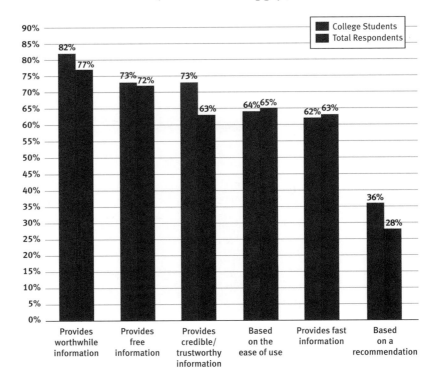

Source: *Perceptions of Libraries and Information Resources,* OCLC, 2005, question 715.

3.2 Judging the Trustworthiness of Information

College students rely on themselves to judge if electronic information is trustworthy, as do total respondents.

College students indicate they use a variety of criteria to select an electronic resource. As noted earlier, 73 percent of college students indicate that *providing credible, trustworthy information* is a key evaluation criterion.

To understand more about the criteria used to judge the trustworthiness of electronic information, respondents who selected this criterion were asked to indicate how they judge trustworthiness. Eighty-three percent of college students indicate they use *personal knowledge/common sense* to determine trustworthiness. Three other criteria were selected by over half of college student respondents. These include the ability to *find the information on multiple sites/cross-reference* (71 percent), the *reputation of the company/organization* (69 percent) and *recommendation from a trusted source* (68 percent). Only 2 percent of college students indicate that electronic information is trustworthy because *it costs money.*

Factors in Determining Trustworthiness of Information—
by College Students and Total Respondents

How do you judge if electronic information is trustworthy?

Base: Respondents selecting "provides credible/trustworthy information" in question 715.

	College Students	Total Respondents
Based on personal knowledge/common sense	83%	86%
Find the information on multiple sites/cross-referencing	71%	65%
Based on the reputation of the company/organization	69%	75%
Recommendation from a trusted source	68%	59%
Based on the author	46%	26%
Based on the professional appearance of the site	42%	28%
Other	3%	3%
The fact that it costs money	2%	1%

Source: *Perceptions of Libraries and Information Resources,* OCLC, 2005, question 725.

a conduit for information to the general public and a reliable, trustworthy source

47-year-old graduate student from Canada

Source: *Perceptions of Libraries and Information Resources,* OCLC, 2005, question 810, "What do you feel is the main purpose of a library?"

3.3 Trust in Library Resources and Search Engines

Libraries and search engines both provide trustworthy information according to college students.

College students' levels of belief in both the trustworthiness and lack-of-trustworthiness of libraries is higher than that of overall respondents. More than half of college students (53 percent) believe information from search engines is at the same level of trustworthiness as library information. In contrast, 69 percent of total respondents feel that information from a search engine is at the same level of trustworthiness as a library information source.

Roughly a third or more of college students believe that the library's sources are more trustworthy than that of Ask.com, Google, Yahoo! and search engines in general. Twenty-two percent of total respondents believe that information received from a library is more trustworthy than information received from a search engine. Note that even though use varies considerably among brands of search engines (see Part 1), the level of trustworthiness among Ask.com, Google and Yahoo! is nearly equal.

Sixteen percent of college students and 9 percent of all respondents indicated they believe library sources are less trustworthy than search engines.

Trustworthiness of Library Sources vs. Search Engines—
by College Students and Total Respondents

Thinking about your usage of your library and the things you like and dislike about it, is the information you get from the library sources more or less trustworthy compared to the information you can get from search engines?

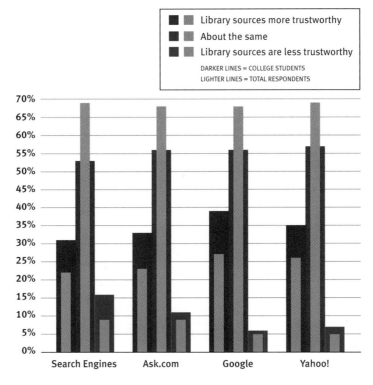

Source: *Perceptions of Libraries and Information Resources,* OCLC, 2005, question 1205.

> ## *A library is vital in order to get information. I trust and love libraries. The web cannot take over because the library is sacred.*
>
> ### 18-year-old undergraduate from the United States

Source: *Perceptions of Libraries and Information Resources,* OCLC, 2005, question 810, "What do you feel is the main purpose of a library?"

3.4 Free vs. For-Fee Information

88 percent of college students have not paid for information or content from an electronic information source.

The survey examined another aspect of trust by asking if respondents trust an electronic information source more if they have to pay for the information. Ninety percent of college students do not trust information they have to purchase more than they trust free information. Similarly, 92 percent of the total respondents said they do not trust the information more if they pay for it.

Free vs. For-Fee Information—
by College Students

Would you trust an electronic information source more if
you have to pay for the information compared to a free source?

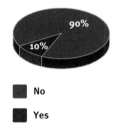

■ No

■ Yes

Source: *Perceptions of Libraries and Information Resources,* OCLC, 2005, question 755.

Paying for Information Via an Electronic Information Source

The survey asked respondents to indicate if they have ever paid for information or content from an electronic information source. Eighty-eight percent of college students report they have not.

Of the college students who have purchased information or content (12 percent), a third or more have purchased a registration to a Web site, audiobooks, articles or subscriptions (48 percent, 39 percent, 37 percent and 33 percent, respectively).

Results for total respondents are similar. Eighty-seven percent of total respondents indicated they have not paid for information or content. Of those who have, nearly a third or more have purchased a registration to a Web site, a subscription or an article (51 percent, 38 percent and 26 percent, respectively).

Free borrowing

22-year-old undergraduate from the United Kingdom

Source: *Perceptions of Libraries and Information Resources,* OCLC, 2005, question 807, "What is the first thing you think of when you think of a library?"

Free vs. For-Fee Information—
by College Students

Have you ever paid for information from an
electronic information source? What did you buy?

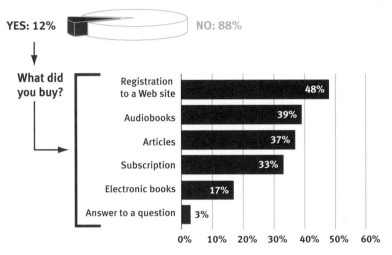

Source: *Perceptions of Libraries and Information Resources*, OCLC, 2005, 625 and 630.

The survey also asked respondents who have purchased information from an
electronic information source if the future frequency of purchasing would be more,
less or about the same. More than half of the college students report they will
purchase information from an electronic information source less frequently, at
56 percent.

In contrast, 59 percent of the total respondents report frequency of purchasing
information will remain the same, 25 percent say frequency will be less and 16
percent say frequency will be more.

Information Purchases in the Future—
by College Students and Total Respondents

Do you anticipate you will be paying more frequently, less frequently or
at about the same frequency for electronic information in the future?

Base: Respondents indicating they have purchased information from an
electronic information source listed in question 625.

	College Students	Total Respondents
More frequently	4%	16%
About the same	40%	59%
Less frequently	56%	25%

Source: *Perceptions of Libraries and Information Resources*, OCLC, 2005, question 635.

Free vs. For-Fee Verbatim Comments

Would you trust an electronic information source more if you have to pay for the information compared to a free source?

College students provided 266 comments to an open-ended question asking why they would or would not trust an electronic source more if they had to pay for the information. Responses indicate a wide range of perceptions and expectations with regard to for-fee information. Some feel that for-fee information is more likely to be trustworthy because it is likely more scrutinized prior to release. Others feel that because so much free information is readily available, it is hard to justify any payment and payment for information typically would be considered a scam.

The traditional notion that higher price equals higher quality appears not to hold true for information as a commodity. There is a clear theme expressed through the comments that information should be free and available to all.

Note: All verbatim comments presented as entered by survey respondents, including spelling, grammatical and punctuation errors.

Because it is more likely to be accurate and truthful, while anyone can make a website and put any information on it even if it's not accurate.
21-year-old undergraduate from the United States

I'm not sure the website would still be trustworthy regardless of if it costs money. I'd also base it on the appearance of the site, credibility in the author, and also it would depend on how the website gets my money (paypal, etc).
20-year-old undergraduate from the United States

It most likely comes from a journal or other source where they have editors who choose which information to sell. They would lose money if people discover the information is false.
22-year-old undergraduate from the United States

Because the web is a place where anyone who wants to make a quick buck can write a good ad & charge people money to access information. I'd be more likely to pay money for information through more traditional channels, such as print media etc.
38-year-old graduate student from Australia

Payment is no guarantee of quality.

44-year-old graduate student from Canada

information should not include price. Knowledge is free and therefore should be to all people. However, pay sites most likely do so because they need to offset the cost of the putting the information together at first.
38-year-old graduate student from Canada

Having to pay for a source does not guarantee it will be a reputable source of information.
50-year-old graduate student from the United States

I find that most of the information I get is from free sources. I would pay if I needed an archived article (and I had no other way of obtaining it) but not for a search. Maybe for a highly specialized search (although I would use my librarian first)...
35-year-old graduate student from India

Payment for service means little. Look at the new Google Scholar service it is an excellent resources for study.
43-year-old undergraduate from Australia

3.5 Validating Information

78% of college students rely on their teachers/ professors for validation.

College student respondents most often cross-reference other Web sites to validate electronic information.

Seventy-one percent of college student respondents judge the trustworthiness of electronic information sources by *cross-referencing to other sources* (see Part 3.2).

The survey explored cross-referencing as a method of information validation. Survey respondents were given a list of possible cross-referencing sources and asked to select all that apply.

More than a third of college students (36 percent) use a *librarian* as a method for validation. *Other Web sites with similar information* was their top choice for validation, at 80 percent, followed closely by *teachers/professors,* at 78 percent. Seventy-six percent of college students also rely on *print materials,* 64 percent on *library materials,* and 59 percent rely on an *expert in the field of interest* as sources for validation.

Librarians are rated as the least-used cross-referencing source for validation among total respondents at 16 percent. Over 80 percent of total respondents use *other Web sites with similar information* as a validation tool. *Print material* is selected as a cross-reference source by 68 percent of total respondents.

Cross-referencing Sources to Validate Information—
by College Students and Total Respondents

What other source(s) do you use to validate the information?
(Select all that apply.)

Base: Respondents selecting "find the information on
multiple sites/cross-referencing" in question 725.

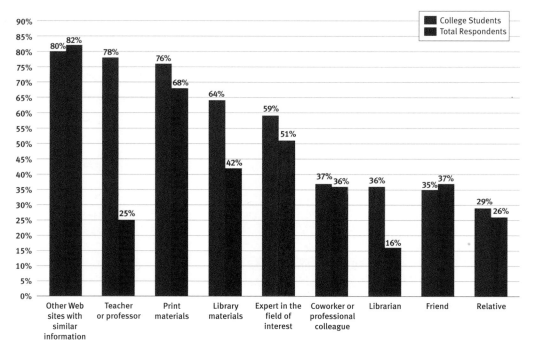

Source: *Perceptions of Libraries and Information Resources*, OCLC, 2005, question 735.

Trusted Sources for Recommendations

Teachers/professors are the top trusted sources college students use for validating information. Two percent consult librarians when seeking help from a trusted source.

While 71 percent of college students judge the trustworthiness of electronic resources by *finding information on multiple sites/cross-referencing,* 68 percent indicate they use *recommendations from a trusted source.* We asked this subset of respondents to identify who or what is their most trusted source they typically use. Nine options were provided and respondents were asked to select one. Forty-five percent of college students use a *teacher/professor* as the trusted source to help judge if electronic information is trustworthy, eclipsing any other response by a factor of at least three. The next most used source, *other Web sites with similar information,* is used by 15 percent of college students. *Librarians* were selected as a trusted source for validating information by 2 percent of college students.

While 65 percent of total respondents judge the trustworthiness of electronic resources by *finding the information on multiple sites/cross-referencing*, 59 percent of total respondents indicate they use *recommendations from a trusted source*. Nineteen percent of this subset of respondents use an *expert in the field of interest* as the trusted source they typically use to help judge if electronic information is trustworthy. Like the college student responses, *librarians* were selected as a trusted source for validating information by 2 percent of total respondents.

Trusted Sources for Validating Information—
by College Students and Total Respondents

Who or what is that trusted source you most typically use?

Base: Respondents selecting "recommendation from a trusted source" in question 725.

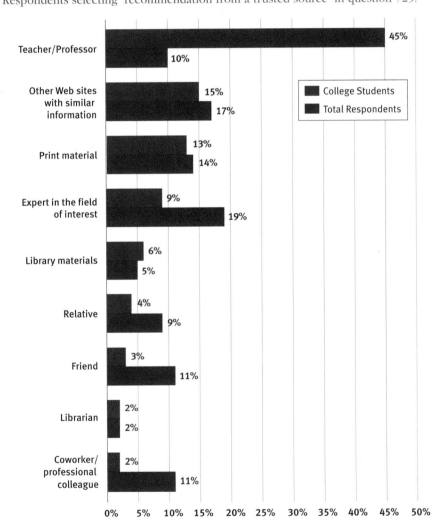

Source: *Perceptions of Libraries and Information Resources*, OCLC, 2005, question 745.

Hard copies of materials easy to navigate

Ability to cross reference and photocopy

43-year-old undergraduate from Australia

Source: *Perceptions of Libraries and Information Resources*, OCLC, 2005, question 812a, "Please list two positive associations with the library."

3.6 Libraries—Positive and Negative Associations

"Books" and "information" are the highest positive associations college students have with libraries. "Books" and "materials" yielded the highest number of negative associations.

Survey respondents were asked to provide—in their own words—two positive and two negative associations about libraries. Responses from 364 college students yielded 638 positive comments (an average of 1.75 comments per respondent) and 363 college students provided 611 negative comments (an average of 1.68 comments per respondent).

Responses from 3,034 total respondents yielded 5,271 positive comments (an average of 1.74 comments per respondent) and 2,985 total respondents provided 4,793 negative comments (an average of 1.61 comments per respondent).

Verbatim responses were grouped into four categories: Products and Offerings, Facility/Environment, Staff and Customer/User Service. These primary categories were used to group both positive and negative associations. As the following graph indicates, respondents' positive and negative comments are matched across the four categories. Respondents had strong positive associations with products and offerings; respondents also had strong negative associations with products and offerings.

Both positive and negative associations were remarkably consistent between college students surveyed and respondents in general.

Books are heavy and you may only need a small amount of information.

30-year-old undergraduate from the United Kingdom

Source: *Perceptions of Libraries and Information Resources*, OCLC, 2005, question 812b, "Please list two negative associations with the library."

Positive and Negative Associations of Libraries—
by College Students and Total Respondents

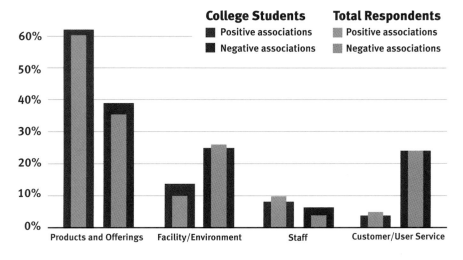

Please list two positive and two negative associations with the library.

Source: *Perceptions of Libraries and Information Resources*, OCLC, 2005, question 812.

Positive Associations

Note: All verbatim comments presented as entered by survey respondents, including spelling, grammatical and punctuation errors.

large variety of
resource material
free

50-year-old graduate student
from Australia

Source: *Perceptions of Libraries and Information Resources*, OCLC, 2005, question 812a, "Please list two positive associations with the library."

Free resources
and books

Free databases
and Internet

48-year-old undergraduate
from Canada

Source: *Perceptions of Libraries and Information Resources*, OCLC, 2005, question 812a, "Please list two positive associations with the library."

Products and Offerings

Books: 18 percent of college student respondents provided positive associations related to books. These comments included free books, many or a variety of books, borrowing books, good books, available or accessible books and browsing books.

Information: 16 percent of college student respondents included positive thoughts related to information, including free information, accurate/ trustworthy information, reliable information, access to information, current information and comprehensive information.

Materials: 8 percent of college student respondents offered comments associated with library materials, such as a variety or many materials available, free materials and borrowing materials.

Free: 8 percent of the college student respondents have positive associations related to the concept of "free" or "free access."

Resources: 5 percent of the positive associations were associated with access to free or a variety of resources.

Computers: 3 percent of the positive comments related to computer or Internet access.

Easy to access/find: 3 percent of the college student respondents provided positive statements about the ease of accessing or finding information or resources.

books! books!
19-year-old undergraduate from the United States

being able to access information free of charge having a
large number of specialized books available.
24-year-old graduate student from Canada

lots of information available
range of materials (books, persiodicals etc).
22-year-old graduate student from the United Kingdom

They give people access to books that they could not afford to
go to the store and buy. They allow people who can not afford a
computer to use the one at the library.
22-year-old undergraduate from the United States

The diversity of information available.
The amount of information.
20-year-old undergraduate from the United States

Positive Associations (cont.)

Facility/Environment

13 percent of the college student respondents have positive associations of the library related to the:

- Quiet environment
- Friendly and comfortable surroundings
- Work environment

Quiet environment and easy access to research material
24-year-old graduate student from the United States

A good place to get information and a good place to study
20-year-old undergraduate from the United States

nice atmosphere
a place to go to get needed information
21-year-old undergraduate from Canada

Staff

9 percent of college student respondents provided positive comments related to the library staff, including:

- Helpful
- Friendly
- Knowledgeable

amount of information
assistance of librarian
19-year-old undergraduate from Australia

hands on data
librarian help
22-year-old undergraduate from the United States

Large selections of books and availability
of knowledgable staff to help find information
19-year-old undergraduate from the United States

Friendly Staff
Meeting like minded readers
51-year-old undergraduate from the United Kingdom

rich in resources
peaceful
atmosphere
conducive to
concentration

55-year-old graduate student from the United States

Source: *Perceptions of Libraries and Information Resources*, OCLC, 2005, question 812a, "Please list two positive associations with the library."

Helpful librarians, and it has everything and if it doesn't they can get it for you.

19-year-old undergraduate from the United States

Source: *Perceptions of Libraries and Information Resources*, OCLC, 2005, question 812a, "Please list two positive associations with the library."

Positive Associations (cont.)

Public access
Lots of
information

**49-year-old graduate student
from Canada**

Source: *Perceptions of Libraries and
Information Resources,* OCLC, 2005,
question 812a, "Please list two positive
associations with the library."

Customer/User Service

4 percent of the college student respondents have positive associations of the service provided by libraries. Some of the positive associations are:

- The practice of being open to the public
- The online catalog
- Interlibrary loan and library "linking"
- The way libraries are organized
- Libraries meet respondents' needs

Fun to search for information
23-year-old undergraduate from the United States

online catalog reserve books, music, tapes/dvd's
20-year-old undergraduate from the United States

Provides a central location of different types of information.
Easily accessible
18-year-old undergraduate from the United States

Comprehensive resource
Knowledgeable librarians to check

35-year-old graduate student from Singapore

good catalogue
lots of journals
25-year-old graduate student from the United Kingdom

Provides many services and products for free or cheaper than they would for the individual. Provides a wide variety of resources for people who would otherwise not have access to them.

20-year-old graduate student from Australia

Negative Associations

Note: All verbatim comments presented as entered by survey respondents, including spelling, grammatical and punctuation errors.

Products and Offerings

Books: 13 percent of the college student respondents had negative associations with library books, including that they are:

- Not available
- Difficult to access
- Heavy to carry
- Not what is needed
- Not current
- Not taken care of or are dirty
- Of limited variety
- Having to wait for books to be returned

Other comments suggested that there are too many books and that the respondents have to return the books to the library.

Materials: 12 percent of the negative comments related to library materials, including:

- The limited variety
- Are hard to access/find/use
- Are not what is needed
- Are not circulated
- Not available
- Are not current
- Are not taken care of/dirty

Information: 7 percent of the college student respondents made negative comments regarding information, including:

- Hard to access/find/use
- Not available
- Too much
- Not current
- Not what is needed
- Limited variety

Computers: 3 percent of the college student respondents have negative associations regarding:

- Outdated computers
- Computers that are not available

Time-consuming: 4 percent of college student respondents made negative comments indicating that use of the library is time-consuming.

Having to travel to get to the library. Sometimes poor condition of books and magazines

19-year-old undergraduate from the United States

Source: *Perceptions of Libraries and Information Resources*, OCLC, 2005, question 812b, "Please list two negative associations with the library."

Dated materials. May not have materials considered non-mainstream.
50-year-old graduate student from the United States

INFORMATION NOT ALWAYS AVAILABLE, BOOKS NOT UPDATED REGULARLY
49-year-old graduate student from Canada

books are heavy and you may only need a small amount of information
30-year-old undergraduate from the United Kingdom

Negative Associations (cont.)

Doesn't always have what you want. Limited availability.

20-year-old undergraduate from the United States

not a wide selection, sometimes material is not up to date on research subjects

20-year-old undergraduate from the United States

Not enough computer in here. Lack of new books for kids.

18-year-old undergraduate from the United States

*time consuming
hard to find*

23-year-old undergraduate from the United States

*Have to actually go into the library
Takes alot of time to search through all the books*

18-year-old undergraduate from the United Kingdom

distance to travel to (incurs time and money implications) not open in the evenings

53-year-old undergraduate from the United Kingdom

Source: *Perceptions of Libraries and Information Resources*, OCLC, 2005, question 812b, "Please list two negative associations with the library."

Facility/Environment

12 percent offered negative comments about the library environment, including:

- Too quiet
- Limited parking
- Confusing layout
- Too noisy
- Too small
- Homeless people
- Too crowded
- Dirty
- Outdated

Travel there: 7 percent of college student respondents have negative associations with travel to the library.

Dull: 4 percent of the college student respondents indicated that libraries are dull.

Not convenient: 2 percent of the college student respondents commented that the library is not convenient.

*Old-fashioned
Boring*

20-year-old graduate student from the United States

*nerd's hangout
dull, boring places*

19-year-old undergraduate from Canada

*Uncomfortable chairs
A long, drawn-out process*

21-year-old undergraduate from Canada

Having to physically go to the location to borrow a book or find the information. They are not open all the time.

19-year-old undergraduate from the United States

Negative Associations (cont.)

Customer/User Service

23 percent of the college student respondents provided negative associations related to:

- Limited or poor hours of operation
- Fees and policies associated with using the library
- Stringent return dates and other limits on circulation
- Use of the online catalog
- Poor service
- Waiting in line
- Lack of privacy

Strict rules.
Overdue fees.

**21-year-old undergraduate
from the United States**

Source: *Perceptions of Libraries and Information Resources*, OCLC, 2005, question 812b, "Please list two negative associations with the library."

need to pay fees to gain access to books/articles/journals
only extract of books are available
40-year-old graduate student from Singapore

overdue costs
short due dates
49-year-old graduate student from Canada

1. You are limited to access of the informaiton by the library's hours of operation 2. There may not be a library convienient to you.
30-year-old undergraduate from the United States

Fees for late books. Renewal of cards.
21-year-old undergraduate from the United States

Staff

6 percent of the college student respondents indicated negative associations related to the library staff, including:

- Unfriendly
- Not knowledgeable
- Unavailable
- Not helpful

unhelpful staff

sometimes difficult to get your hands on the information you need because somebody else has the books out

**21-year-old undergraduate
from Canada**

Source: *Perceptions of Libraries and Information Resources*, OCLC, 2005, question 812b, "Please list two negative associations with the library."

hard to navigate, difficult to find knowledgeable help
21-year-old graduate student from the United States

the libraries that I have been to have librarians that don't like to help. They expect you to figure out where the book is that you are looking for and don't like using the card catalog.
21-year-old undergraduate from the United States

3.7 Lifestyle Fit

College students are reading less and using the library less since they started using the Internet.

Watching television, using the library, reading books, reading magazines and *purchasing music* are the top five activities students report doing less frequently since they began using the Internet. Seventeen percent of college student respondents report their activities have not decreased since they began using the Internet. Fourteen percent of college student respondents say they *visit with family and friends* less often.

39%
of college students **use the library** *less since they began using the Internet.*

Decreased Activities Due to Internet Use—
by College Students and Total Respondents

What activities do you engage in less often since you began using the Internet?
(Select all that apply.)

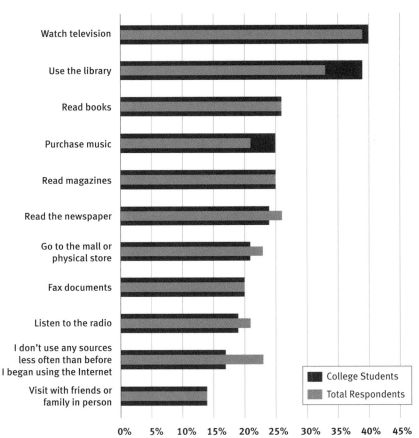

Source: *Perceptions of Libraries and Information Resources*, OCLC, 2005, question 415.

Information Sources and Lifestyle Fit

Nearly two-thirds of college students say search engines fit perfectly with their lifestyles.

Understanding how compatible a product or service is to a consumer's lifestyle and consumption habits can provide interesting insights into how a consumer may use that product or a competing product or service in the future.

Respondents rated search engines, libraries, online libraries, bookstores and online bookstores as information sources that did, or did not, fit with their lifestyle.

College students are more likely than respondents in general to rate information sources as fitting perfectly within their lifestyle. Whether rating search engines, libraries, online libraries, bookstores or online bookstores, college students are comfortable with information sources as part of their lifestyle. Sixty-three percent of college students rate both online and physical libraries as having a good to perfect fit for their lifestyle, while less than 50 percent of total respondents do so.

While college students rate libraries significantly higher than all respondents do, college students still rate search engines higher than they do libraries, with 94 percent indicating that search engines are a good to perfect lifestyle fit, which is similar to the response from total respondents at 90 percent.

Information Sources by Lifestyle Fit—
by College Students

Thinking of each information source and your information needs and lifestyles, would you say it...?

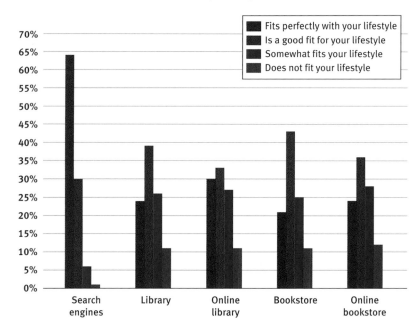

Source: *Perceptions of Libraries and Information Resources*, OCLC, 2005, question 1345.

Information Sources with Perfect Lifestyle Fit—
by College Students and Total Respondents

Thinking of each information source and your information needs and lifestyles, would you say it *fits perfectly with your lifestyle?*

	College Students	Total Respondents
Search engines	64%	55%
Library	24%	17%
Online library	30%	15%
Bookstore	21%	14%
Online bookstore	24%	16%

Source: *Perceptions of Libraries and Information Resources*, OCLC, 2005, question 1345.

Online Libraries and Lifestyle Fit

Although both information sources are Internet-based, substantially more respondents rate search engines as a perfect fit than online libraries. Thirty percent of college students indicate the online library fits perfectly with their lifestyles, while 64 percent indicate search engines are a perfect fit with their lifestyles.

Fifteen percent of total respondents say the online library fits perfectly with their lifestyles. Fifty-five percent rate search engines as a perfect fit.

Online Libraries Compared to Search Engines—
by College Students

Thinking of each information source and your information needs and lifestyles, would you say it...?

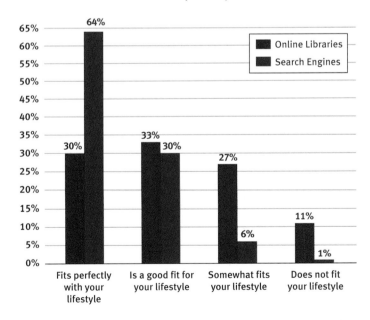

Source: *Perceptions of Libraries and Information Resources*, OCLC, 2005, question 1345.

3.8 Books—the Library Brand

The library brand is books.

Books and research
22-year-old undergraduate from Canada

a place to find all kinds of books
19-year-old undergraduate from the United States

Book Heaven!
21-year-old undergraduate from the United States

BOOKS
32-year-old undergraduate from the United Kingdom

books, books, and more books
40-year-old undergraduate from Australia

Lovely, lovely books! The complete package!
26-year-old undergraduate from Australia

lots of books!!
47-year-old graduate student from Canada

Books!
35-year-old graduate student from India

Borrowing books
29-year-old graduate student from Singapore

lots of books free
23-year-old graduate student from the United Kingdom

In the introduction to this report, we noted that one of the most important goals of the project is to begin to provide a clearer understanding of the "Library" brand. In this section, we consider what the library brand might mean to college student respondents.

"Brand" is derived from the Old Norse word "brandr," which means "to burn," as brands were the means by which owners of livestock marked their animals to identify them.[1] The American Marketing Association defines "brand image" as "the perception of a brand in the minds of persons. The brand image is a mirror reflection (though perhaps inaccurate) of the brand personality or product being. It is what people believe about a brand—their thoughts, feelings, expectations."[2]

We asked a variety of questions in this survey to help us collect information about the library's brand image and about the respondents' thoughts, feelings and expectations.

---

1. Kevin Lane Keller, *Strategic Brand Management: Building, Measuring and Managing Brand Equity*, (Upper Saddle River, NJ: Prentice Hall, Inc., 1998), 2.
2. http://www.marketingpower.com/mg-dictionary.php?Searched=1&SearchFor=brand%20image (accessed October 15, 2005).

We asked the open-ended question: "What is the first thing you think of when you think of a library?" A total of 3,785 verbatim comments were provided from 3,163 total respondents and were grouped by main theme. Of the total, 396 verbatim comments were contributed by 384 college students. About 70 percent of total respondents, as well as 70 percent of college students, associate "library" first and foremost with books. There was no runner-up.

First (Top-of-mind) Association with the Library— *by College Students and Total Respondents*

What is the first thing you think of when you think of a library?

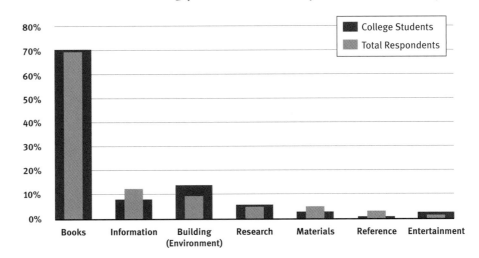

Source: *Perceptions of Libraries and Information Resources,* OCLC, 2005, question 807.
Note: The percentage is based on the number of comments received divided by the number of respondents. Some respondents chose to provide more than one response, and all responses were included.

Books, i love all the books. To pick up a book and hold it in my hand is still a really cool feeling.

27-year-old undergraduate from the United States

Source: *Perceptions of Libraries and Information Resources,* OCLC, 2005, question 807, "What is the first thing you think of when you think of a library?"

Brand Associations

The open-ended responses from the 3,163 total respondents and 384 college students were also analyzed for secondary themes or descriptors that could lend understanding of library brand image. The words "book" or "books" were mentioned 261 times by college students, and the word "information" was the top-of-mind recall 26 times among college students.

Among total respondents, the words "book" or "books" were mentioned 2,152 times and the word "information" was the top-of-mind recall 291 times. Other descriptors mentioned infrequently included access, the physical building, the librarian and library as "a place for information," but the overwhelming response is that the library brand equals books.

Words often used by librarians to describe libraries and library services include "trust," "privacy," "authoritative," "quality," "education" and "learning." We reviewed 396 verbatim comments from 384 college students to the question "What is the first thing you think of when you think of a library?" to see how many times "trust," "privacy," "authoritative," "quality," "education" and "learning" were mentioned by college student respondents. The words "trust," "privacy" and "authoritative" were never mentioned by college students. "Quality" was mentioned once. "Education" was mentioned once; "learning" was mentioned three times. "Books" were mentioned 261 times.

	Top-of-Mind Library Associations	
	College Students	Total Respondents
Books	261	2152
Information	26	291
Quality	1	2
Education	1	4
Learning	3	9
Free	5	70

So why the overwhelming brand image of library as books?

As mentioned in the introduction, *Environmental Scan* discussions with librarians over the past two years have often surfaced a view that a potential reason for the disconnect between the user's perception of libraries as books and the librarian's association with a much broader set of products and services is a lack of user education. Many have expressed a feeling that today's information consumer is just not aware of what is currently available at libraries. The survey data would support the assertion that library users (aside from college students) are not aware of many electronic library resources.

As reported in Part 2.2, total respondents are unaware or unfamiliar with many of the products and services currently available at the library. Although college students have more awareness of library electronic resources than respondents overall, many are not sure what libraries offer. Thirty-two percent of college student respondents are not sure that their libraries offer electronic journals. Thirty-one percent are not sure that their libraries provide online databases. Twenty-three percent are not sure if their libraries have online reference materials.

Why are respondents so uninformed? Ninety percent of college student respondents hold a library card, and 72 percent of all respondents hold a library card.

A Sample of College Students' Verbatim Comments:
What is the first thing you think of when you think of a library?

Note: All verbatim comments presented as entered by survey respondents, including spelling, grammatical and punctuation errors.

Books.
What else?

18-year-old undergraduate
from the United States

deadlines
19-year-old undergraduate from the United States

Almost all kinds of resources can be found there.
21-year-old undergraduate from Singapore

Book Heaven!
21-year-old undergraduate from the United States

Dust
22-year-old undergraduate from the United States

easily accesing to informations on line,
the availability of books, journals ect..
28-year-old graduate student from the United Kingdom

books books and more books
40-year-old undergraduate from Australia

Good resource, but may not always have the resource available
at that moment when we need it urgently.
35-year-old graduate student from Singapore

Happiness...I love the library!
All that knowledge in one place.
27-year-old graduate student from the United States

shhhhh
39-year-old undergraduate from Canada

having to search throuh many books
to find relevant information
19-year-old undergraduate from Australia

A Sample of College Students' Verbatim Comments (cont.):
What is the first thing you think of when you think of a library?

Note: All verbatim comments presented as entered by survey respondents, including spelling, grammatical and punctuation errors.

I think of a large selection of books and magazines of all topics as well as having access to online journals and other online information sources
19-year-old undergraduate from the United States

Lovely, lovely books! The complete package!
26-year-old undergraduate from Australia

Outdated and lame.
18-year-old undergraduate from the United States

research and studying
20-year-old undergraduate from Canada

Silence and being bored.
20-year-old undergraduate from the United States

Useful librarians
18-year-old undergraduate from the United States

A wonderful resource filled to the brim with glorious books...such a wealth of knowledge.
24-year-old undergraduate from the United States

be quiet
39-year-old undergraduate from the United States

lots of books!!
47-year-old graduate student from Canada

3.9 Brand Potential—Libraries, Books and Information

The majority of respondents indicated that the main purpose of libraries was broader than books.

To provide useful information for research and knowledge
21-year-old undergraduate from the United States

*A place to read peacefully,
gather information*
22-year-old undergraduate from the United States

An institution that disseminates knowledge
23-year-old undergraduate from the United States

Collect human knowledge
45-year-old undergraduate from Canada

Entertainment and research
19-year-old undergraduate from Australia

Education and fun
22-year-old graduate student from the United Kingdom

As important as it is to know what your brand image is today, it is equally important to understand brand potential. What are the possibilities? Can brand image be changed or expanded? Can brand image be "refreshed?" What potential exists for expanding the "Library" brand beyond books?

To explore "Library" brand potential, we asked respondents to look beyond first impression and indicate what they felt is the purpose (mission) of the library.

Nearly half (49 percent) of college students and 53 percent of all respondents indicated that they feel the main purpose of the library is information. Thirty-three percent of college students and 31 percent of respondents indicated that the main purpose of the library is books.

Main Purpose of the Library—
by College Students and Total Respondents

What do you feel is the main purpose of the library?

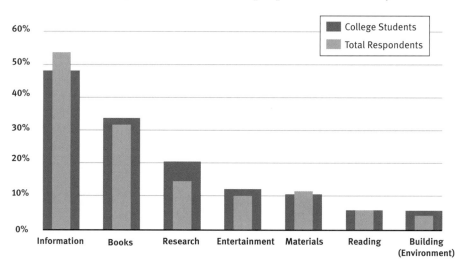

Source: *Perceptions of Libraries and Information Resources*, OCLC, 2005, question 810.

For Learning, enjoyment, interacting with people, obtaining latest releases, able to get other than books eg. DVD'S videos, Information, contact point.

40-year-old undergraduate from the United Kingdom

Responses to the question "What do you feel is the main purpose of the library?" varied in both content and length. Some responses were one- or two-word replies; others were lengthy answers indicating more than one main purpose of the library.

Responses such as "to allow the public the option to freely educate themselves or entertain themselves" (21-year-old undergraduate from the United States) indicate a multidimensional view of the purpose of the library. Free, educate and entertainment are all mentioned. The majority of respondents indicated that their view of the main purpose of the library was broader than just books. When books were mentioned, other activities or services were also frequently mentioned.

	Main Purpose of the Library Word Count	
	College Students	Total Respondents
Books	124	1019
Information	144	1290
Quality	0	4
Education	19	87
Learning	14	91
Free	36	253

The data suggest that, when prompted, many respondents can see a role for libraries beyond books.

A Sample of College Students' Verbatim Comments:
What do you feel is the main purpose of the library?

Note: All verbatim comments presented as entered by survey respondents, including spelling, grammatical and punctuation errors.

free access to information and entertaining reading
22-year-old graduate student from the United States

provide access to information
20-year-old graduate student from the United States

providing information i.e books
29-year-old graduate student from Australia

To offer patrons access to knowledge
55-year-old graduate student from the United States

to provide free information
21-year-old graduate student from the United States

To provide information in a systematic way, and to allow patrons to borrow printed and non-printed material as needed
35-year-old graduate student from India

*A library is vital in order to get information.
I trust and love libraries. The web cannot take over because the library is sacred.*
18-year-old undergraduate from the United States

A place that holds published information. A place where people can go to search for and locate information of a particular subject.
18-year-old undergraduate from Australia

access to books, both informative and for enjoyment
21-year-old undergraduate from the United States

entertainment and research
19-year-old undergraduate from Australia

I think the main purpose of a library is to provide everyone with the means to print documents and information.
19-year-old undergraduate from Canada

information/ research/ lending books
24-year-old undergraduate from the United States

A Sample of College Students' Verbatim Comments (continued):
What do you feel is the main purpose of the library?

Note: All verbatim comments presented as entered by survey respondents, including spelling, grammatical and punctuation errors.

place of research and place where people can study
22-year-old undergraduate from Australia

provide solid information from all sources
21-year-old undergraduate from the United Kingdom

*PROVIDE USE OF BOOKS AND KNOWLEDGE THAT IS NEEDED
AND QUIET ARE FOR PEOPLE THAT NEED TO STUDY*
32-year-old undergraduate from the United Kingdom

Providing informational materials to the community
22-year-old undergraduate from the United States

Serve as a centralized information repository
21-year-old undergraduate from the United States

To keep me from going crazy, I am a book nut.
51-year-old undergraduate from Canada

to provide a vast amount of books and information that can be found in one place with some kind of order

18-year-old undergraduate from the United States

Part 4: College Students' Advice to Libraries

Keep up the good job
27-year-old undergraduate from Australia

renovation needed to improve the building to make it more accomodating to study
21-year-old graduate student from the United States

need a bigger work space
47-year-old graduate student from Canada

Train librarians to be more friendly and helpful
22-year-old graduate student from the United Kingdom

Respondents were asked to indicate their level of agreement with a set of phrases and characteristics to determine how they see the library's role in today's society. When prompted, respondents *completely agree* or *agree* that libraries serve many community roles, including a place to learn, a place to read and support literacy, a place for free computer/Internet access and a place to promote childhood learning and development.

Respondents were also asked to rate their library service across six service dimensions ranging from librarian assistance to technology. Less than 25 percent of all respondents, including college students, *completely agree* that libraries meet their needs on any single dimension.

As the wrap-up to the survey, respondents were offered the opportunity to provide— in their own words—one piece of advice to libraries. We received 371 responses from college students.

4.1 College Student View:
The Library's Role in the Community

*When prompted, college students agree that
libraries serve many community roles.*

Respondents were asked to rate the library on 14 attributes that describe potential
community roles that a library could provide. Fifty percent or more of college
students and total respondents *completely agree* or *agree* that their library provides
12 of the 14 community services surveyed.

College student responses were similar to that of total respondents when asked to
respond to the statement the library *is a place to learn*. Eighty-six percent of college
students and 85 percent of all respondents *completely agree* or *agree* that the library
is a place to learn.

Eighty percent or more of all respondents also agree *(completely agree* or *agree)* that
the library is a *place to read* and *makes needed information freely available*. These
results were similar to those of the college student respondents, with 81 percent
agreeing *(completely agree* or *agree)* that the library *is a place to read* and 79 percent
agreeing *(completely agree* or *agree)* that the library *makes needed information freely
available*.

Fifty percent of college students *completely agree* or *agree* that their library *promotes
childhood learning and development,* while 73 percent of total respondents
completely agree or *agree* with that statement.

86%
*of college
students at
least agree
their library
is a place
to learn.*

The Library's Role in the Community—
by College Students

Please rate the degree to which you agree or disagree with the following statements about your library's role in the community.

Note: This graph shows the *completely agree* and *agree* responses.

to provide services to the community like books and computers and resorses for everyone not just people who can pay for them.

23-year-old undergraduate from the United States

Source: *Perceptions of Libraries and Information Resources,* OCLC, 2005, question 810, "What do you feel is the main purpose of the library?"

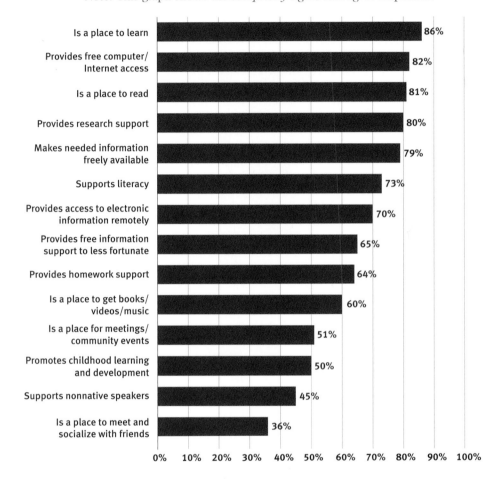

Is a place to learn	86%
Provides free computer/Internet access	82%
Is a place to read	81%
Provides research support	80%
Makes needed information freely available	79%
Supports literacy	73%
Provides access to electronic information remotely	70%
Provides free information support to less fortunate	65%
Provides homework support	64%
Is a place to get books/videos/music	60%
Is a place for meetings/community events	51%
Promotes childhood learning and development	50%
Supports nonnative speakers	45%
Is a place to meet and socialize with friends	36%

Source: *Perceptions of Libraries and Information Resources,* OCLC, 2005, question 1210.

4.2 Rating Library Services

Seventy-five percent of college student respondents at least agree that assistance from a librarian is available when needed.

Seventy-seven percent at least agree that library technology meets their needs.

The survey asked respondents to rate their library's performance across six service dimensions ranging from librarian support to content to resource availability. Nearly two-thirds or more of college students *completely agree* or *agree* that all six service dimensions meet their needs.

Seventy-five percent of college students and 65 percent of total respondents *completely agree* or *agree* that *assistance from a librarian is available when needed.* Seventy-seven percent of college students and 54 percent of total respondents at least agree that library *technology meets their needs.*

A larger percentage of college students than total respondents agree *(completely agree* or *agree)* that the *content/collection meets their needs.* Seventy-two percent of college students agree that the library's collection meets their needs, while 52 percent of total respondents agree.

Librarian and Library Services—
by College Students

Please rate the degree to which you agree or disagree with the following statements about your library.

Note: This graph shows the *completely agree* and *agree* responses.

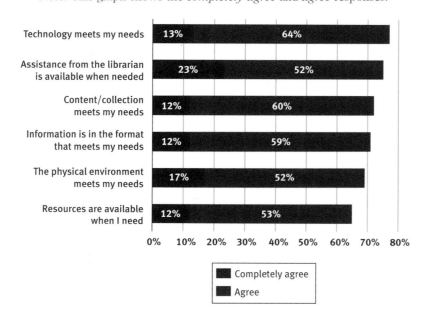

Source: *Perceptions of Libraries and Information Resources,* OCLC, 2005, question 1207.

4.3 Advice to Libraries

College students had opinions on all aspects of library staff, products and services, and facilities.

Listen to patron requests!

19-year-old undergraduate from the United States

Source: *Perceptions of Libraries and Information Resources*, OCLC, 2005, question 1240, "If you could provide one piece of advice to your library, what would it be?"

Respondents were invited to offer one piece of advice to libraries as a wrap-up to the survey. Some respondents offered more than one piece of advice and others declined to comment. We received 371 pieces of advice from college students out of over 3,000 overall advice comments. The advice covered a wide range of topics across a wide range of library services. We categorized the advice into the following five themes: products and offerings, customer/user service, facility/environment, staff and satisfaction.

Advice for the Library— by College Students and Total Respondents

If you could provide one piece of advice to your library, what would it be?

Note: This graph shows the percentage of respondents who offered advice related to the following themes: products and offerings, customer/user service, facility/environment, staff and satisfaction.

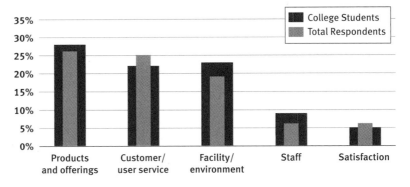

Source: *Perceptions of Libraries and Information Resources*, OCLC, 2005, question 1240.

keep up the good work!

18-year-old undergraduate from the United States

Source: *Perceptions of Libraries and Information Resources*, OCLC, 2005, question 1240, "If you could provide one piece of advice to your library, what would it be?"

College Students' Advice

If you could provide one piece of advice to your library, what would it be?

Note: All verbatim comments presented as entered by survey respondents, including spelling, grammatical and punctuation errors.

Products and Offerings

Add to collection: 12 percent of college student respondents advised libraries to add material to their collections.

Update collection: 7 percent of college student respondents suggested that libraries update their collections with new books, materials, information and other resources.

Computers: 7 percent of college student respondents advised that libraries should increase the number of computers or update them.

Online catalog: 2 percent of college student respondents suggested improvements to the local library system.

My public library needs to expand its horizons and add more books that appeal to more people.

19-year-old undergraduate from the United States

Source: *Perceptions of Libraries and Information Resources,* OCLC, 2005, question 1240, "If you could provide one piece of advice to your library, what would it be?"

classify databases according to faculty. improve the search function of databases. improve signage/layout. extend the size of the room for group meetings (quiet talking and food and drinks allowed)
19-year-old undergraduate from Australia

Get more current information and new books in there.
19-year-old undergraduate from the United States

Increase the amount of new titles. Bring in DVDs etc and videos of academic need.
29-year-old undergraduate from Canada

Allow personal wireless cards for use on library network
44-year-old graduate student from the United States

Get electronic access to older back issues of academic journals or take them out of the annex and put them back in the stacks.
27-year-old graduate student from the United States

Subscribe to more electronic journals
24-year-old graduate student from Canada

College Students' Advice (cont.)

Customer/User Service

Service: 14 percent of college student respondents provided advice related to libraries' services.

Promote: 2 percent of college student respondents suggested increasing libraries' promotional efforts.

Access: 6 percent of college student respondents advised libraries to increase accessibility to the physical library, as well as to electronic resources.

don't direct every-one to the card catalog....get up and help them

21-year-old undergraduate from the United States

Source: *Perceptions of Libraries and Information Resources,* OCLC, 2005, question 1240, "If you could provide one piece of advice to your library, what would it be?"

Free copiers
20-year-old undergraduate from the United States

library website for info and renewing books
42-year-old undergraduate from the United Kingdom

More borrowing time
20-year-old undergraduate from Australia

Setting up a physical library at major offices can be good.
35-year-old graduate student from Singapore

It could be a bit more accessible for independent use by mobility impaired users
50-year-old graduate student from Australia

Longer opening hours
29-year-old graduate student from Australia

open up earlier in the morning so that i can use the facility before my morning classes
21-year-old undergraduate from the United States

To email details of local events happening to readers who may be interested especially in events happening in association with the library.
51-year-old undergraduate from the United Kingdom

College Students' Advice (cont.)

Facility/Environment

23 percent of college student respondents provided advice related to the physical library environment or facility.

Let us eat and drink in the library..or at least designated study areas instead of no food or drink anywhere
19-year-old undergraduate from Canada

Cleaner bathrooms
18-year-old undergraduate from the United States

It is always very cold and this makes the environment very unpleasant
21-year-old undergraduate from the United States

Do something about the bums and transients
24-year-old undergraduate from the United States

Regulate temperature better for comfort
35-year-old graduate student from the United States

Some table lamps would be nice
23-year-old undergraduate from the United States

better atmosphere, more tables to do work on...a lot were eliminated when computers were added (computers are nice but more tables are needed for group work)
22-year-old graduate student from the United States

Arrange seating so students can NOT sit in clusters and socialize. Library is for studying, not socializing
44-year-old graduate student from Canada

Update the look a little bit so it's easier to find things other than the tape on the floor
19-year-old undergraduate from the United States

Change the fluro lighting. It's a health hazard
29-year-old undergraduate from Australia

Get a snack bar
21-year-old graduate student from Canada

Get more comfortable chairs, tables, and meeting spaces so people actually want to go there

18-year-old undergraduate from the United States

Source: *Perceptions of Libraries and Information Resources*, OCLC, 2005, question 1240, "If you could provide one piece of advice to your library, what would it be?"

College Students' Advice (cont.)

Staff

9 percent of college student respondents provided advice regarding library staff.

Be friendly and helpful to students
23-year-old undergraduate from the United States

Friendlier librarians and assistants
20-year-old undergraduate from the United States

More staff would be helpful
57-year-old graduate student from Canada

Hire a nicer staff
19-year-old undergraduate from the United States

Be much more student friendly
23-year-old undergraduate from Australia

friendlier staff
22-year-old graduate student from the United States

More librarians who aren't snotty
20-year-old undergraduate from the United States

Train librarians to be more friendly and helpful
22-year-old graduate student from the United Kingdom

Hire people who really want to be there and will be friendly and readily available to help students who ask for help.

29-year-old undergraduate from Canada

Source: *Perceptions of Libraries and Information Resources*, OCLC, 2005, question 1240, "If you could provide one piece of advice to your library, what would it be?"

College Students' Advice (cont.)

Satisfaction

5 percent of college student respondents indicated they were satisfied with the library and the services offered.

Continue to support education and literacy among the community
19-year-old undergraduate from the United States

Great job! Need more computers, though
19-year-old undergraduate from the United States

good work
19-year-old undergraduate from Australia

I can't think of anything, the library is great
32-year-old undergraduate from the United States

It is a very friendly place
21-year-old undergraduate from Canada

Keep it alive!
19-year-old undergraduate from the United States

Nothing. I think that my college library is very well kept. They have the latest information and technology and they have very helpful staff on hand.
19-year-old undergraduate from the United States

None. It is a good library
43-year-old graduate student from the United States

Keep keeping up! You are an invaluable resource/facility in the community. Without you, many people's opportunity/desire to learn & develop would be greatly diminished (think Billy Connelly & Michael Caine's love of libraries)
26-year-old undergraduate from Australia

Part 5: Perceptions of Potential College Students

U.S. respondents in the 14- to 17-year-old age group provide a comparison with responses from worldwide college students. College students of the near future will potentially come from this group, and so it is interesting to note the differences and similarities in perceptions of libraries and their resources between this group and those already attending colleges.

The majority of young people who responded to the survey reside in the U.S. In the original report, data from all U.S. respondents were segmented by age to provide yet another perspective on the data. The sample sizes of respondents from the other geographic regions were not large enough to report by age segment.

Usage of libraries among U.S. 14- to 17-year-olds is higher than among other U.S. age segments:

- 83 percent are current library card holders

- 58 percent use their school library at least on a monthly basis

- 34 percent visit the public library at least monthly

- 35 percent reported an increase in library use in the past three to five years

The data suggest that the younger respondents use newer types of electronic resources more readily than older respondents. Usage of the following five electronic resources is higher among this younger U.S. segment than among college students worldwide: instant messaging/online chat, e-mail information subscriptions, blogs, ask an expert services and online librarian question services.

However, while U.S. 14- to 17-year-olds frequently use electronic resources, only 20 percent who have used a library Web site *completely agree* it provides worthwhile information compared to 45 percent of worldwide college students who *completely agree*.

Additional differences are evident related to valued and trusted sources. Seventy-five percent of worldwide college students *completely agree* or *agree* that librarians add value to the search process, compared to 51 percent of U.S. 14- to 17-year-olds. This younger segment relies on friends and relatives as cross-referencing tools more so

---

58%

of U.S. 14- to 17-year-olds visit their school library at least monthly.

---

get newer books,

better computers,

more staff

15-year-old high school student from the United States

Source: *Perceptions of Libraries and Information Resources*, OCLC, 2005, question 1240, "If you could provide one piece of advice to your library, what would it be?"

than worldwide college students. U.S. 14- to 17-year-olds are also slightly more likely to trust information from a source where a fee is required compared to total U.S. respondents and worldwide college students.

U.S. 14- to 17-year-olds report a higher agreement level than worldwide college students on the following two of 14 roles a library contributes to a community:

- *Promotes childhood learning and development*
- *Is a place to meet and socialize with friends*

41% *of U.S. 14- to 17-year-olds anticipate their library usage will increase, nearly double that of total U.S. respondents.*

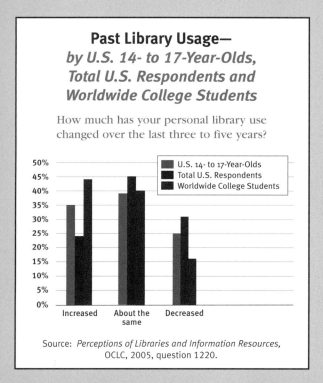

Past Library Usage—
by U.S. 14- to 17-Year-Olds, Total U.S. Respondents and Worldwide College Students

How much has your personal library use changed over the last three to five years?

- U.S. 14- to 17-Year-Olds
- Total U.S. Respondents
- Worldwide College Students

Source: *Perceptions of Libraries and Information Resources,* OCLC, 2005, question 1220.

Anticipated Future Library Use—
by U.S. 14- to 17-Year-Olds, Total U.S. Respondents and Worldwide College Students

How do you anticipate your personal usage of the library will change over the next three to five years?

- U.S. 14- to 17-Year-Olds
- Total U.S. Respondents
- Worldwide College Students

Source: *Perceptions of Libraries and Information Resources,* OCLC, 2005, question 1225.

Get more funding. Newer books are needed in some areas, and the outside of the building could use some new paint.

15-year-old high school student
from the United States

Source: *Perceptions of Libraries and Information Resources,* OCLC, 2005, question 1240, "If you could provide one piece of advice to your library, what would it be?"

To stop spending money on tables and chairs and to spend it on getting newer books and information to the students.

14-year-old high school student
from the United States

Source: *Perceptions of Libraries and Information Resources,* OCLC, 2005, question 1240, "If you could provide one piece of advice to your library, what would it be?"

It is possible that when the U.S. 14- to 17-year-olds enter college, their perceptions will more closely match those of the college student respondents. But it is also possible that the responses of the U.S. 14- to 17-year-olds represent a generational difference and that they will continue to place less value on librarians and to use library resources less.

The verbatim comments provided by people in this age group show many of them feel a lack of respect and acceptance from library staff, and this could impact their perceptions of libraries as well as influence their future use of libraries and their resources.

Be more student friendly

16-year-old high school student
from the United States

Source: *Perceptions of Libraries and Information Resources*, OCLC, 2005, question 1240, "If you could provide one piece of advice to your library, what would it be?"

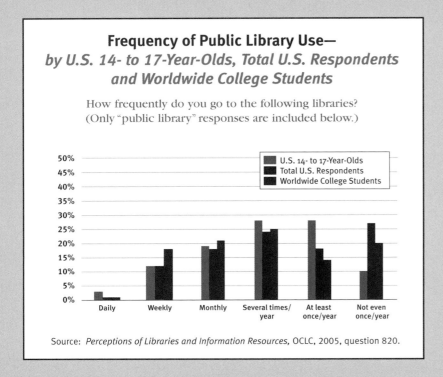

Frequency of Public Library Use—
by U.S. 14- to 17-Year-Olds, Total U.S. Respondents and Worldwide College Students

How frequently do you go to the following libraries?
(Only "public library" responses are included below.)

Legend:
- U.S. 14- to 17-Year-Olds
- Total U.S. Respondents
- Worldwide College Students

Source: *Perceptions of Libraries and Information Resources*, OCLC, 2005, question 820.

34%
of U.S. 14- to 17-year-olds visit their public library at least monthly.

Keep books up to date and have more teen friendly environments

15-year-old high school student
from the United States

Source: *Perceptions of Libraries and Information Resources*, OCLC, 2005, question 1240, "If you could provide one piece of advice to your library, what would it be?"

Improve the web site more—I like the catalog, but if it could reference some sort of rating system it would be even better—I was looking at a new author today who has many books, and I had to go to an internet computer, check on amazon and see which books were most highly recommended, and go back to the catalog to see if they were available.

15-year-old high school student
from the United States

Source: *Perceptions of Libraries and Information Resources*, OCLC, 2005, question 1240, "If you could provide one piece of advice to your library, what would it be?"

Be more friendlier

14-year-old high school student from the United States

Source: *Perceptions of Libraries and Information Resources*, OCLC, 2005, question 1240, "If you could provide one piece of advice to your library, what would it be?"

Have the librarians seem more approachable, less stiff and imposing.

16-year-old high school student from the United States

Source: *Perceptions of Libraries and Information Resources*, OCLC, 2005, question 1240, "If you could provide one piece of advice to your library, what would it be?"

Librarians Add Value to the Search Process—
by U.S. 14- to 17-Year-Olds, Total U.S. Respondents and Worldwide College Students

Please rate the degree to which you agree or disagree that the librarian adds value to the information search process.

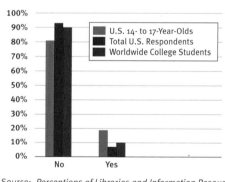

Source: *Perceptions of Libraries and Information Resources*, OCLC, 2005, question 1070.

Free vs. For-Fee Information—
by U.S. 14- to 17-Year-Olds, Total U.S. Respondents and Worldwide College Students

Would you trust an electronic information source more if you have to pay for the information compared to a free source?

Source: *Perceptions of Libraries and Information Resources*, OCLC, 2005, question 755.

Usage of Electronic Resources—
by U.S. 14- to 17-Year-Olds, Total U.S. Respondents and Worldwide College Students

Please indicate if you have used the following electronic information sources, even if you have used them only once.

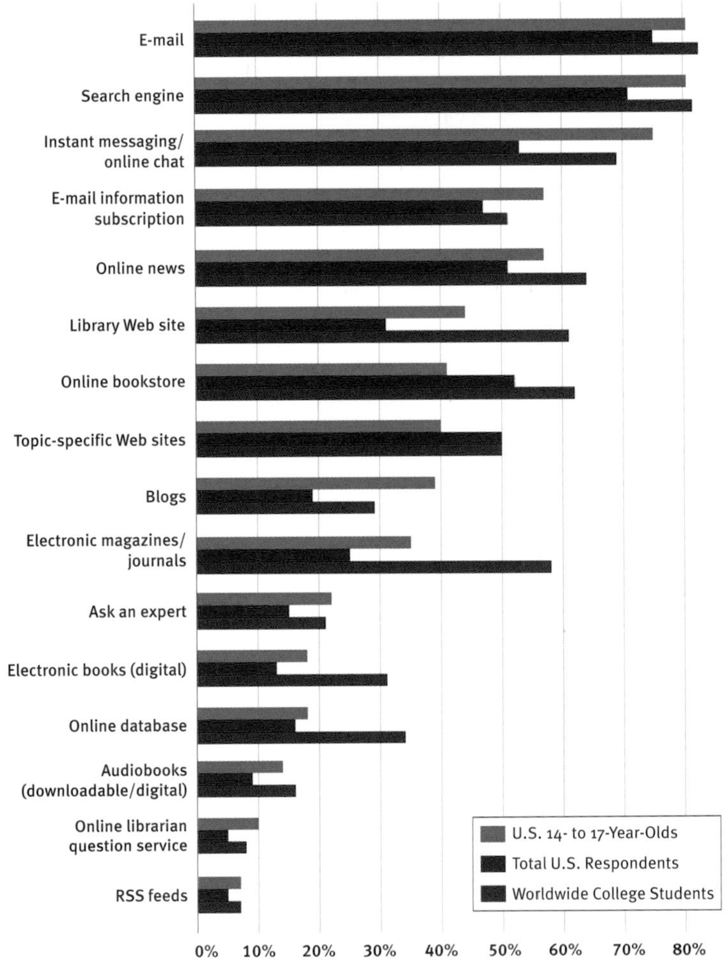
E-mail
Search engine
Instant messaging/ online chat
E-mail information subscription
Online news
Library Web site
Online bookstore
Topic-specific Web sites
Blogs
Electronic magazines/ journals
Ask an expert
Electronic books (digital)
Online database
Audiobooks (downloadable/digital)
Online librarian question service
RSS feeds
U.S. 14- to 17-Year-Olds
Total U.S. Respondents
Worldwide College Students
0%
10%
20%
30%
40%
50%
60%
70%
80%

Source: *Perceptions of Libraries and Information Resources,* OCLC, 2005, question 505.

Have a display for interesting books.

16-year-old high school student from the United States

Source: *Perceptions of Libraries and Information Resources,* OCLC, 2005, question 1240, "If you could provide one piece of advice to your library, what would it be?"

75%

of U.S. 14- to 17-year-olds have used instant messaging.

more computer stations, able to bring in your own computer and hook up to internet

17-year-old high school student from the United States

Source: *Perceptions of Libraries and Information Resources,* OCLC, 2005, question 1240, "If you could provide one piece of advice to your library, what would it be?"

Cross-referencing Sources to Validate Information—
by U.S. 14- to 17-Year-Olds, Total U.S. Respondents and Worldwide College Students

What other source(s) do you use to validate the information?

Base: Respondents selecting "find the information on multiple sites/cross-referencing" in question 725.

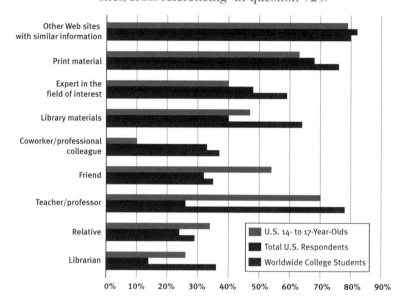

Source: *Perceptions of Libraries and Information Resources*, OCLC, 2005, question 735.

encourage reading for FUN instead of just for school and stop placing traditional high school literature in such high regard over other books

17-year-old high school student from the United States

Source: *Perceptions of Libraries and Information Resources*, OCLC, 2005, question 1240, "If you could provide one piece of advice to your library, what would it be?"

provide snacks and drinks

16-year-old high school student from the United States

Source: *Perceptions of Libraries and Information Resources*, OCLC, 2005, question 1240, "If you could provide one piece of advice to your library, what would it be?"

69% *of U.S. 14- to 17-year-olds agree the library is a place to learn.*

Worthwhile Information from the Library Web site—
by U.S. 14- to 17-Year-Olds, Total U.S. Respondents and Worldwide College Students

Please rate the degree to which you agree or disagree that each electronic information source provides worthwhile information.

(Only *Completely Agree* responses are graphed below.)
Base: Respondents who indicated usage of the library Web site from a list of 21 information brands.

U.S. 14- to 17-Year-Olds	20%
Total U.S. Respondents	34%
Worldwide College Students	45%

0% 5% 10% 15% 20% 25% 30% 35% 40% 45%

Source: *Perceptions of Libraries and Information Resources*, OCLC, 2005, question 670.

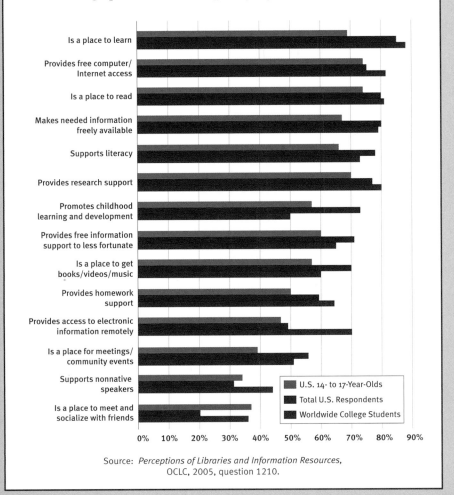

Library's Role in the Community—
by U.S. 14- to 17-Year-Olds, Total U.S. Respondents and Worldwide College Students

Please rate the degree to which you agree or disagree with the following statements about your library's role in the community.

Note: This graph shows the *completely agree* and *agree* responses.

Is a place to learn
Provides free computer/ Internet access
Is a place to read
Makes needed information freely available
Supports literacy
Provides research support
Promotes childhood learning and development
Provides free information support to less fortunate
Is a place to get books/videos/music
Provides homework support
Provides access to electronic information remotely
Is a place for meetings/ community events
Supports nonnative speakers
Is a place to meet and socialize with friends

■ U.S. 14- to 17-Year-Olds
■ Total U.S. Respondents
■ Worldwide College Students

0% 10% 20% 30% 40% 50% 60% 70% 80% 90%

Source: *Perceptions of Libraries and Information Resources,* OCLC, 2005, question 1210.

Alert visitors when their book is close to overdue. And automatically renew a book if there is no one else with that book on reservation.

16-year-old high school student from the United States

Source: *Perceptions of Libraries and Information Resources,* OCLC, 2005, question 1240, "If you could provide one piece of advice to your library, what would it be?"

More computers and better advertising for new books

15-year-old high school student from the United States

Source: *Perceptions of Libraries and Information Resources,* OCLC, 2005, question 1240, "If you could provide one piece of advice to your library, what would it be?"

Don't require the library card if the person has an account.

17-year-old high school student from the United States

Source: *Perceptions of Libraries and Information Resources,* OCLC, 2005, question 1240, "If you could provide one piece of advice to your library, what would it be?"

Have more special events to bring people into the library and advertise them well.

16-year-old high school student from the United States

Source: *Perceptions of Libraries and Information Resources,* OCLC, 2005, question 1240, "If you could provide one piece of advice to your library, what would it be?"

have a longer business hour on friday, saturday and Sunday

15-year-old high school student from the United States

Source: *Perceptions of Libraries and Information Resources*, OCLC, 2005, question 1240, "If you could provide one piece of advice to your library, what would it be?"

Provide more activities directed towards teens.

15-year-old high school student from the United States

Source: *Perceptions of Libraries and Information Resources*, OCLC, 2005, question 1240, "If you could provide one piece of advice to your library, what would it be?"

To provide better access and better direction to online resources.

15-year-old high school student from the United States

Source: *Perceptions of Libraries and Information Resources*, OCLC, 2005, question 1240, "If you could provide one piece of advice to your library, what would it be?"

update-make it look newer and hipper. also some of the books are musty so that makes it smell bad

15-year-old high school student from the United States

Source: *Perceptions of Libraries and Information Resources*, OCLC, 2005, question 1240, "If you could provide one piece of advice to your library, what would it be?"

To have a separate room for completely silent study.

16-year-old high school student from the United States

Source: *Perceptions of Libraries and Information Resources*, OCLC, 2005, question 1240, "If you could provide one piece of advice to your library, what would it be?"

Keep it up, I appreciate everything you do.

16-year-old high school student from the United States

Source: *Perceptions of Libraries and Information Resources*, OCLC, 2005, question 1240, "If you could provide one piece of advice to your library, what would it be?"

Make it more approachable to teenagers-Starbucks or something similar would help, as well as nice seating areas.

17-year-old high school student from the United States

Source: *Perceptions of Libraries and Information Resources*, OCLC, 2005, question 1240, "If you could provide one piece of advice to your library, what would it be?"

Have more comfortable furniture for reading in the library. The bookstore has nice couches but the library just has tables and chairs.

17-year-old high school student from the United States

Source: *Perceptions of Libraries and Information Resources*, OCLC, 2005, question 1240, "If you could provide one piece of advice to your library, what would it be?"

> **When cross-referencing, more U.S. 14- to 17-year-olds rely on *library materials and librarians for validation* than total U.S. respondents.**

Conclusion

Libraries, many of their resources and services, and the information experts who work in libraries appear to be increasingly less visible in a universe of abundant information, but without data we could not say with any certainty how extensive this apparent shift has become. The *Perceptions of Libraries and Information Resources* report provides this data.

College students' decreased activities due to Internet use...

40%   Watch TV less

39%   Use the library less frequently

24%   Read the newspaper less

19%   Listen to the radio less

14%   Visit with family/ friends in person less often

College Students' Perceptions of Libraries and Information Resources presents a subset of that data. It includes the responses of 396 survey participants who identified themselves as current attendees of a postsecondary institution. The report also includes a chapter on some of the responses of U.S. survey participants between the ages of 14 and 17 to provide contrast and comparison with the college students, as these young people are potential college attendees of the future.

The purpose of the report is to provide a clear picture of the perceptions of college-attending respondents, for the benefit of academic librarians and their colleagues. The report is the result of a need to better understand the interests, habits and behaviors of college students using libraries—or not—in a time of information abundance.

Data for college students are often presented in comparison with data for the total respondents, but it is important to note that the data for students are a subset of the data for all respondents.

A summary of the findings related to college students as well as a few conclusions and observations follow.

Report Findings

...on College Students' Perceptions and Habits

- College students use **search engines** to begin an information search (89 percent). Two percent begin an information search on a **library Web site**. *(Part 1.2)*

- College students like using search engines. Ninety-three percent were *very satisfied* or *satisfied* with the overall experience of using a search engine compared to 84 percent who expressed the same level of satisfaction with the overall search experience, assisted by a librarian. *(Part 2.6)*

- College students like to self-serve. Many **do not seek assistance** when using library resources (54 percent) although more seek assistance than do respondents overall (46 percent compared to 36 percent). *(Part 2.4)*

- College students indicate a higher level of use of electronic information services than respondents overall. *(Part 1.1)*

...on Libraries

- **College students** have the **highest rate of library use** and broadest use of library resources, both physical and electronic. *(Parts 1 and 2)*

- College students **use the library,** but they use the library less and read less since they began using the Internet. *(Parts 1.1 and 3.7)*

- The most frequent use of the library among college students is as a **place to do homework and study**. *(Part 2.1)*

- "Books" is the **library brand** among college students. There is no runner-up. *(Part 3.8)*

- College students show **high levels of awareness** of library electronic resources. *(Parts 1 and 2)*

- **Only 10 percent** of college students **indicated that their library's collection fulfilled their information needs** after accessing the library Web site from a search engine. *(Part 2.5)*

...on Alternatives to Libraries

- College students use **personal knowledge and common sense** and **cross-referencing other sites** to judge if electronic information is trustworthy. They use other Web sites with similar information and their teachers to validate information. *(Parts 3.2 and 3.5)*

- **Fifty percent** of college students learn about electronic information sources from teachers, 36 percent from a library Web site and 33 percent from a librarian. *(Part 1.3)*

- **Search engines fit** college students' lifestyles better than physical or online libraries. The majority of college students see search engines as a perfect lifestyle fit. *(Part 3.7)*

Conclusions and Observations

What was confirmed and revealed

As discussed briefly in the introductions of the full *Perceptions* report and of this report, many findings of the survey confirm the trends we highlighted in *The 2003 OCLC Environmental Scan*. But what was revealed is that in many areas college students use libraries more, and are more aware of resources, than are respondents overall. Also, when correlations were done between educational attainment and library use, there is evidence that the more educated the respondent, the more likely they are to use libraries after formal education is completed.

These survey results confirm that libraries are used by college students. The number of students holding library cards is higher than among respondents overall: 90 percent of college students hold a library card, while 72 percent of total respondents hold a library card. College students use both academic and public libraries frequently. College students also expect their library usage to increase in the future at a higher rate than do total respondents.

When asked to give advice, many student respondents suggested increasing libraries' open hours, improving the lighting and furniture, hiring friendlier staff and allowing food and drink in libraries. Their verbatim comments reveal ambivalence to the physical library not exposed in the data.

The results confirm that the majority of college students are still not making high use of the array of electronic resources (online magazines, databases and reference assistance, for example) libraries make available. However, college students use electronic resources at higher rates and are the most familiar with what libraries have to offer compared to usage and familiarity of overall respondents.

Results also confirm that respondents are aware that libraries are "wired" and many use the computers in libraries to access the Internet and to use Internet resources. The majority of college students and high school students use library computers regularly.

However, there is widespread high use of general Internet information resources among college students. They regularly use search engines, e-mail and instant messaging to obtain and share information. The library is not the first or only stop for these information seekers. Search engines are the favorite place to begin a search and respondents indicate that Google is the search engine most recently used to begin their searches. Among students who have started a search using a search engine, 48 percent ended up at a library Web site. Forty-one percent went on to use the library Web site, but only 10 percent agreed the library Web site fulfilled their information needs. Twenty-seven percent indicated they also had to use other resources. The results of this survey confirm that libraries are not seen as the top choice for access to electronic resources, even among college students who have the highest level of awareness of those resources.

The survey revealed how college students make choices about electronic information resources and how they evaluate those resources, and make decisions about the

Lots of books to read, free computer access.

27-year-old undergraduate from Australia

Source: *Perceptions of Libraries and Information Resources*, OCLC, 2005, question 812a, "Please list two positive associations with the library."

quality, trustworthiness and monetary worth of resources available from libraries and generally on the open Web. Many college students do not differentiate between what is offered by libraries and what is offered by search engine companies.

While it is easy to assume that search engines are the top choice of information consumers because of the speed with which information can be delivered, the study revealed that speed is not the only, and not the primary, reason search engines are the preferred starting point.

Respondents, including college students, indicated that search engines deliver better quality and quantity of information than librarian-assisted searching—and at greater speed. As more and more content becomes digital and directly accessible via search engines, quantity will increase. The amount of quality information, overall, is also likely to increase.

College students trust information they get from libraries, and they trust the information they get from search engines. The survey revealed that they trust them almost equally, which suggests that libraries have no monopoly on the provision of information.

Most college students are very familiar with search engines, e-mail and instant messaging. As more content becomes directly accessible via search engines and to handheld devices, familiarity with more and different types of digital content is likely to increase. Will trust continue to increase too?

The survey highlighted that not only are college students happy to self-serve, they are confident that they can serve themselves well. When asked how they judge the trustworthiness of information, "common sense/personal knowledge" was the top method used. This self-reliance was also reflected in college students' use of the library. Most say they have not asked for help using any library resources, either at the physical or the virtual library.

As more and more content becomes digital and accessible via the Internet, the number of information sources available for both information discovery and validation is likely to increase, fueling increased confidence and self-reliance.

Survey respondents, including college students, are generally satisfied with libraries and librarians, but many of them, particularly teenagers, use the library less since they began using the Internet. Verbatim comments reveal strong attachments to libraries as places, but many of these positive associations are nostalgic in nature, and are not related to current experiences. Younger respondents—college students and teenagers—did not express these nostalgic associations as frequently, and commented frequently on the negative aspects of physical libraries and their staffs.

While the attachment to the traditional nature and purpose is an asset all libraries share, it is not clear that this attachment extends, or will extend, to virtual libraries and their electronic resources. The data in this report show that libraries lack relevance in the lives of younger respondents, and that their resources and services are not clearly differentiated from other information sources.

Make the library more inviting and update your books.

18-year-old undergraduate from the United States

Source: *Perceptions of Libraries and Information Resources*, OCLC, 2005, question 1240, "If you could provide one piece of advice to your library, what would it be?"

We learned that respondents had much to say, when asked, about their libraries, the people who staff them and the services offered. This suggests that libraries have an opportunity to learn much more than was revealed in this report about the perceptions of the people in their communities by conducting local polls and open-ended surveys. The data serve as a reminder to readers that college students are also heavy users of public libraries. Perhaps this suggests there could be more cooperation among all libraries in a community.

The data revealed that the more educated respondents are, the more they use libraries, even after their formal education is completed. Forty-nine percent of respondents indicating they had college degrees use public libraries or academic libraries at least monthly, compared to 25 percent of high school graduates who use public libraries or academic libraries at least monthly.

The Library Brand

Sitting in the middle of the stacks with books around me, and I am just reading and loving it.

18-year-old undergraduate from the United States

Source: *Perceptions of Libraries and Information Resources*, OCLC, 2005, question 807, "What is the first thing you think of when you think of a library?"

One of the most important goals of the project was to obtain a clearer understanding of the "Library" brand. What do information consumers think about libraries today? How do information consumers identify libraries in the growing universe of alternatives? What is the "Library" brand image?

What is the library's identity in the minds of information seekers? By a huge margin respondents feel that "library" is synonymous with "books." When asked about their first spontaneous impression of libraries, 69 percent of information consumers reply, "books." This is true also of 70 percent of college students.

Familiarity, trust and quality—these are intangible traits often summed up by the word "brand." All brands from search engines to cars to libraries are either familiar or not, trusted or not, provide top quality or not. We tested these brand concepts in the survey.

We asked about familiarity. Libraries are very familiar as book providers. Search engines are very familiar as electronic information providers. We reviewed the concept of trust. The lines are fuzzy. Libraries and search engines are trusted almost equally among college students. We asked about quality. College students see both libraries/librarians and search engines as providers of quality information. Again, the lines are blurred. In a tie, the data suggest the nod would go to search engines.

The "Library" brand is dominant in one category—books. It would be delightful to assume that when respondents say "books," what they really mean to say is that books, in essence, stand for those intangible qualities of information familiarity, information trust and information quality. The data did not reveal it. We looked hard. We reviewed thousands of responses to the open-ended questions that inquired about positive library associations and library purpose. We searched for words and phrases that included mentions of "quality," "trust," "knowledge," "learning," "education," etc. We found mentions of each, but they were relatively few in number. "Books" dominated—across all regions surveyed, across all age groups and among college students.

It is interesting that despite college students' higher use and awareness of libraries and their electronic resources, books are still the main brand associated with libraries.

In addition to being familiar, trusted and high-quality, strong brands must be relevant. Relevance is the degree to which people believe a brand meets their needs. In the survey, we tested for relevancy and lifestyle fit. Sixty-four percent of college students said that search engines perfectly fit their lifestyle. Thirty percent said online libraries are a perfect fit. Eleven percent said libraries do not fit their lifestyle. That library resources and librarians add value to information search was not disputed by respondents, but the data suggest that the relevancy and lifestyle fit of that value are in question.

In a world where the sources of information and the tools of discovery continue to proliferate and increase in relevance to online information consumers, the brand differentiation of the library is still books. The library has not been successful in leveraging its brand to incorporate growing investments in electronic resources and library Web-based services. Can the brand be expanded or updated to be more relevant, to be more than books?

Libraries must work collectively to "rejuvenate" the brand. It is not simply about educating students about the library and its physical and electronic resources. Trying to educate consumers whose habits and lifestyles are changing and have changed seldom works. It doesn't work for companies and it probably won't work for libraries. Rejuvenating the "Library" brand depends on the abilities of the members of the broad library community to redesign library services so that the rich resources—print and digital—they steward on behalf of their communities are available, accessible and used. Rejuvenating the brand depends on reconstructing the experience of using the library. While the need for localized points of distribution for content that is no longer available in just physical form is likely to become less relevant, the need for libraries to be gathering places within the community or university has not decreased. The data are clear. When prompted, information consumers see libraries' role in the community *as a place to learn, as a place to read, as a place to make information freely available, as a place to support literacy, as a place to provide research support, as a place to provide free computer/ Internet access* and more. These library services are relevant and differentiated.

Libraries will continue to share an expanding infosphere with an increasing number of content producers, providers and consumers. Information consumers will continue to self-serve from a growing information smorgasbord. The challenge for libraries is to clearly define and market their relevant place in that infosphere—their services and collections both physical and virtual.

It is time to rejuvenate the "Library" brand.

Continue to support education and literacy among the community. When supporting the backbone of the community (education and literacy) don't be afraid to try new things and new methods.

19-year-old undergraduate from United States

Source: *Perceptions of Libraries and Information Resources,* OCLC, 2005, question 1240, "If you could provide one piece of advice to your library, what would it be?"

About OCLC

OCLC serves 54,000 libraries in 109 countries.

OCLC Online Computer Library Center is a nonprofit membership organization that promotes cooperation among libraries worldwide. More than 54,000 libraries in 109 countries use OCLC services to locate, acquire, catalog, lend and preserve print and electronic library materials.

OCLC was established in Ohio in 1967 by a small group of libraries whose leaders believed that working together they could find practical solutions to some of the day's most challenging issues. What began as a way to automate the traditional library card catalog rapidly became a collaborative revolution that involved thousands of libraries around the world. Working together, OCLC and its member libraries cooperatively produce and maintain WorldCat—the OCLC Online Union Catalog—which now contains over 67 million bibliographic records and more than 1 billion library holdings.

Collaboration among librarians and OCLC solved the practical problem of automated cataloging. Ongoing collaboration led to additional OCLC services, including services that help libraries build e-content collections and provide online access to special library collections like maps, newspapers, photographs and local histories.

The OCLC membership jointly created the largest interlibrary loan system in the world. Recent expansions and new partnerships in Europe now enable the OCLC collaborative to exchange more than 9.5 million items annually to information consumers and scholars around the world.

The library content represented in WorldCat is now accessible to people using major search engines due to the Open WorldCat program that opens up the assets of the OCLC cooperative to the searchers of the world.

In addition to the many services offered, OCLC funds library research programs, library advocacy efforts, scholarships, market research and professional development opportunities.

OCLC Research incubates new technologies, sponsors the work of library scientists and represents libraries on a range of international standards bodies. OCLC Research is also actively engaged with the world's information community to further the science of librarianship.

OCLC library advocacy programs are part of a long-term initiative to champion libraries to increase their visibility and viability within their communities. Programs include advertising and marketing materials to reinforce the idea of the library as relevant, and market research reports that identify and communicate trends of importance to the library profession. Several of the reports are noted in the introduction to this report.

OCLC provides financial support for those beginning their library careers and for established professionals who excel in their endeavors through a series of annual awards and scholarships. Of note is the IFLA/OCLC Early Career Development Fellowship Program, jointly sponsored by the International Federation of Library Associations and Institutions (IFLA), OCLC Online Computer Library Center and the American Theological Library Association (ATLA). The program provides early career development and continuing education for library and information science professionals from countries with developing economies.

OCLC participates in WebJunction, which is an online community of libraries and other agencies that share knowledge and experience to provide the broadest public access to information technology. A service created by the Bill & Melinda Gates Foundation's U.S. Library Program, OCLC and other partners, WebJunction features articles, handouts, courses and forum discussions that are practical, down-to-earth and friendly. WebJunction addresses the real issues that librarians and library staff face every day.

OCLC's vision is to be the leading global library cooperative, helping libraries serve people by providing economical access to knowledge through innovation and collaboration. OCLC is headquartered in Dublin, Ohio, USA and has offices throughout the world.

OCLC Online Computer Library Center
6565 Frantz Road
Dublin, Ohio 43017 USA
www.oclc.org

OCLC Asia Pacific
6565 Frantz Road
Dublin, OH 43017-3395 USA
www.oclc.org/asiapacific/en/

OCLC Canada
701 Salaberry Street, Suite 200
Chambly, Quebec J3L 1R2 Canada
www.oclc.org/ca/

OCLC Latin America and the Caribbean
6565 Frantz Road
Dublin, OH 43017-3395 USA
www.oclc.org/americalatina/en/

OCLC Mexico
Ave. Amores 707 desp.401, Col. Del Valle
03100 Mexico, D.F. Mexico
www.oclc.org/americalatina/en/

OCLC Middle East and India
6565 Frantz Road
Dublin, Ohio 43017 USA
www.oclc.org/middleeast/en/

OCLC PICA Netherlands
Head Office and Service Centre for Netherlands, Belgium, Luxembourg
Schipholweg 99
P.O. Box 876
2300 AW Leiden, The Netherlands
www.oclcpica.org

OCLC PICA United Kingdom
Service Centre for U.K., Northern and Eastern Europe, Southern Africa
7th Floor, Tricorn House,
Birmingham, B16 8TP England
www.oclcpica.org

OCLC PICA France
Service Centre for Southern Europe, Turkey and Israel
14, Place des Victoires
92600 Asnières sur Seine, France
www.oclcpica.org

OCLC PICA Germany
Service Centre for Germany, Austria and Switzerland
c/o Sisis Informationssysteme GmbH
Grünwalder Weg 28g
82041 Oberhaching, Germany
www.oclcpica.org